Caring for the Flock

Four Marks

of the
Healthy Ministry
Professional

John W. Daniels, III
Daniel S. Yearick

Caring
for the
Flock

Four Marks

of the
Healthy Ministry
Professional

John W. Daniels, III
Daniel S. Yearick

HEARTSPRING PUBLISHING
JOPLIN, MISSOURI

Copyright © 2007
College Press Publishing Co.
Toll-free order line 800-289-3300
On the web at www.collegepress.com

Cover design by Brett Lyerla

Library of Congress Cataloging-in-Publication Data

Daniels, John W., 1964–
  Four marks of the healthy ministry professional / by John W.
Daniels III, Daniel S. Yearick.
    p. cm.
  Includes bibliographical references.
  ISBN 978-0-89900-926-1 (softback)
  1. Clergy—Office—Psychological aspects. 2. Clergy—Mental
health. 3. Clergy—Psychology. 4. Clergy—Job stress. 5. Vocation—
Christianity.
I. Yearick, Daniel S., 1961- II. Title.
  BV4398.D36 2007
  253'.2--dc22

                                                    2007014976

Caring for the Flock
Series Introduction

Shepherding evokes idyllic images of green pastures, fluffy sheep, and carefree shepherds lounging in the grass. But shepherding is not all lazy days spent by a babbling brook. Shepherding involves hard work; in fact it can be downright demanding. The sheep, unfortunately, do not possess an enormous amount of intelligence, and they find themselves quite often in need of the shepherd's care and assistance. So the shepherd spends his days watching for predators, caring for injuries, searching for strays, delivering newborn lambs, and directing his flock to the right pastures.

It is in these images that God chose to communicate not only how He cares for us, but also how church leaders are to care for the church. We see in the New Testament admonitions to "be shepherds of God's flock," "be examples to the flock," and "keep watch over yourselves and all the flock." And the very word that Ephesians 4:11 labels "pastor" finds its roots in the Greek word for shepherd. God's people are led by modern-day shepherds, and while you won't see a minister extracting thorns from a member's wool or directing the Sunday school class with a staff and rod, he performs the same types of tasks. Preachers, elders, deacons, ministry leaders are frequently seen counseling a grieving widow, teaching from God's Word, or celebrating a baptism. It is through the everyday tasks of church life that leaders exercise care for their flocks.

We want to spur your growth as a shepherd. The goal of this

series is to encourage spiritual wholeness, the development of leaders, and counseling skills. As you minister to your congregation, you will face situations that stretch and challenge you, so you will find these books a concise and ready reference. It is our desire that the Caring for the Flock Series will help address the needs and concerns every shepherd faces.

To our wives,

Melinda Daniels

&

Grace Yearick

Acknowledgments

We would like to thank the many ministers and their families whom we have known, both personally and professionally, for their willingness to share not only their struggles *with,* but also their passion *for* the task of The Kingdom.

For editorial assistance, we would like to thank Kathleen Elliott, Executive Director of Agape Counseling Associates, Inc., Rochester, New York; Sara Jenkins of Present Perfect Books, Lake Junaluska, North Carolina; and Jonah Yearick, Chapel Hill, North Carolina.

We express our gratitude to Jessica Scheuermann and the folks at College Press Publishing. It was their encouragement, patience, and willingness to recognize our vision for this book that has made its publishing a reality.

Table of Contents

Introduction

This book addresses the disturbing fact that the success of those in the ministry often comes at the expense of the person God created them to be. We not only expect our ministry leaders to meet our expectations, but often demand that they meet those expectations in exactly the way we want them to be met. We have encountered countless clergy who seem to have a common trait: *Those who enter a career in professional ministry have qualities that make them vulnerable to losing their identity in Christ to their identity as a leader.* Simply put, they no longer live life as who they are, but rather as what they do. Often this manifests as various familiar complaints: feeling worn out, purposeless, out of touch with God, and disconnected from their spouses, questioning their faith, in serious moral trouble, hypocritical, and burned out.

> **They no longer live life as who they are, but rather as what they do.**

We have come to believe that all such ministry professionals need to address the same four issues in order to be emotionally and spiritually whole. These four issues are:

✠ They have unresolved issues relating to family of origin.
✠ They have a distorted or otherwise unhealthy concept of "call" that led to their entering the ministry.

✠ They allow themselves to be spread too thin and believe that their profession does not allow them to set boundaries.

✠ They are lonely, understanding neither the limits nor benefits of relationships.

This book is not about the people, with their problems and their expectations, who fill church pews week after week. Rather it is an honest look at how many ministers' *reactions* to those people originate in the well of emotional issues that they bring with them into their professions. We would not want anyone reading this book to lose his/her passion for ministry. We are, however, asking the reader to examine, and maybe even question, his or her call for the purpose of deepening its reality and its effect on how we live our lives day to day.

The process of examination, the resulting insights, and the recommendations given here are offered out of our concern for ministry professionals. Our own questioning grew out of the friendship between the two of us—not from a therapeutic relationship, even though Dan is a professional counselor who has worked with clergy for more than twenty years. We believe that presenting two perspectives, the personal and the professional, sheds a brighter light on the common struggles of those in ministry, and thus at times we will speak in our individual voices.

The Courage to Begin

John and I (Dan) had been casual friends for about a year. Then, in 1998 there was a moment marked by awkwardness so strong you would have thought we were strangers. John stopped by to leave his daughter with mine for the afternoon. His parting words as he got into his car were, "I could use a little time on your couch sometime." Though he was not literally asking for my professional counseling services, this was the best way he could let me know that he was suffering. The awkwardness was evidence to me that asking for help required John to muster a tremendous amount of courage. That day was not only the beginning of a major healing for him, but also the birth of my deepest friendship.

After making a cross-country move, my family and I became members of the church where John serves as associate pastor. It was our common interest in working with adolescents that first connected the two of us as friends. After a couple of lunches together, the deeper, more real things in common dimmed the glaring differences in our personalities. I became very aware of his uniqueness and felt a definite prompting to give something to him. I did not share this with him, or anyone. Instead I began to pray for him. That moment in the driveway on that September Saturday afternoon became the moment in time when I knew what that earlier prompting meant.

John is a gifted individual who has been called to God. He entered the ministry with a list of personal successes, talents, and a heart overshadowed by another list of emotional wounds. He discovered that he could ignore the pain and sense of failure in life as long as he worked hard at "doing"—capitalizing on his God-given blessings and gifts and by pleasing those he served. However, he eventually became aware of the fact that if he stopped "doing" for one minute, or if the "doing" did not produce spectacular results, then the flood of pain and sense of failure would catch up to him. That moment in my driveway was the point when he realized he was tired and couldn't keep running. Sound like anyone you know?

In spite of the hundreds of people around him, including his colleagues in ministry, John felt very much alone and in need of a real friend in the deepest sense of the word. I believe that those in the ministry sell themselves short regarding the need for friendships. The belief is prevalent that a pastor is a giver, never needing to be given to or ministered to. John's story proves that this is untrue.

> **Those in the ministry sell themselves short regarding the need for friendships.**

A Life Changed

Writing this book is perhaps the most daring task of my ministry. I must claim it; it's my story. It's about call, ministry, passion, emotional health, and the truths (or notions we believe to be truths) about serving the local church. I dare to say that those in ministry who feel persecuted are perhaps those in need of having their beliefs challenged. In essence, if you are in the ministry and feel persecuted by those in your ministry, you may be more culpable for allowing others to "persecute" you than you believe. My belief is that we allow, permit, and enable ourselves to be embattled, often the result of our own personal issues. This is what I hope to describe in the pages of this book.

I do not have a miraculous testimony. I have never used drugs, gambled, been unfaithful to my wife, or belonged to a motorcycle gang. I accepted God's directing to full-time Christian vocation during high school. I achieved all of the standard accolades of a church-raised "you'll be a great preacher someday" kid. I went to a Christian college, traveled the country with a musical team, and spent my summers doing missions or internships. After marriage I attended seminary and graduated in 1991. I have been serving my current church since 1994.

This book comes out of a personal struggle to answer the question, "Who am I?" I must confess that I have lived a life of defining myself as the sum of what I do. My courage to write this book comes from the realization that many, if not all, clergy serve out of a longing to find definition or meaning to life.

We the ordained may be a bigger part of the problem than we would ever dare admit. There are traits pervasive among ministry professionals that lead to a less than fulfilling ministry, personal self-doubt and degradation, family crisis, unhealthy coping mechanisms, and eventual burn-out. This book will address these traits, examine the progression into unhealthy living, and offer hope for healing to both minister and ministry.

> There are traits pervasive among ministry professionals that lead to a less than fulfilling ministry.

Using my life as a model of unhealthiness in the ministry, we will address each of the marks of a healthy ministry professional. The four marks of the healthy ministry professional are:

✠ He or she has addressed and resolved issues relating to his or her family of origin.

✠ He or she has examined his or her "call" and has an understanding of the biblical perspective of "call."

✠ He or she has learned to set and maintain boundaries.

✠ He or she understands the limits of most relationships and embraces and values deep friendships.

We believe this approach offers hope for healing to all clergy who are willing to take a serious inventory of their lives and calling. I am a testimony to this hope.

The Burden of Unresolved Issues

If you cannot get rid of the family skeleton,
you may as well make it dance.
George Bernard Shaw

The purposes of a man's heart are deep waters,
but a man of understanding draws them out *(Prov 20:5)*.

The Identity Formed in Childhood

The premise in counseling theory that our adult lives are influenced by childhood events makes the exploration of our family of origin essential to self-knowledge. The process of examining both positive and negative aspects of our family experience can be threatening, grueling, and painful. But it is in those aspects that we can discover the keys to understanding what motivates us as adults.

Down the sidewalk and across the viaduct to the football practice field ran the mighty warrior—a skinny kid named Johnny. His ankles were no bigger around than silver dollars, and his shoulder pads, draped in his father's worn shirt, hit against his scrawny neck when he ran, for even the smallest size was way too big for him. Against the odds, Johnny was ready for battle—but the battle for a gridiron victory was in truth a fight for his identity and worth in the eyes of his beloved father.

This scared kid was willing to endure the rigors of football because his father had burned into his brain the manly mantra that "quitters never win." Johnny did hang in there for the entire season, but he never played football again. Somehow he sensed even then that pursuing football, which he did not enjoy, to fulfill his father's dream of being an All-American athlete, would never happen.

This vignette reveals the emotional foundation underlying John's later life in the ministry. Much of our personality is formed by the time we are five years of age. This does not mean that by kindergarten we are solidified in our personhood. We are able to make adaptations as we age if we know how, and certainly other life events that occur as we age impact our identity. Nonetheless, our early experiences have a strong bearing on the adults that we become, and it is understanding our early years that enables us to make changes that lead to a healthy adulthood.

Those who study family systems believe that the role we play in one system will be the same role we play in all other systems. For example, if it is your role to be the peacekeeper in your family, you will probably be the peacekeeper in your circle of friends, in your job, in school, and in church. This role is unwittingly developed early in life as a result of factors affecting the family at the time of a child's birth and development. For example, a mother's health crisis may require that a six-year-old take care of younger siblings.

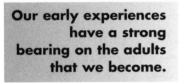

Our early experiences have a strong bearing on the adults that we become.

To better understand John—how his assumed family role has impacted his call to ministry and the way he does ministry—it helps to look at his family of origin to find what role he played there and what factors formed his personhood early in life.

John's Story

My parents were in college when they married. My father was twenty-one years old and a basketball player; my mother was eighteen-years old and a cheerleader. A few months before they married, I was conceived.

When I think about my conception, I feel sickened. It's not that I think sex is dirty and disgusting; I just know that what my parents did when they conceived me was wrong. I've gradually come to admittance—without feeling damned—that I am an illegitimate child (emotionally if not legally). I can see now that my whole life has been spent trying to prove my legitimacy, and deep inside I fight against the belief that my very being was initiated out of an act of sin.

Ouch! It stings to write that. I fear proclaiming that my conception was "sin" implies that I'm passing judgment upon my parents. I'm not, but the truth of their behavior remains. I am not saying that I was an unloved child; I've never doubted the love of my parents, but their actions resulted in a rough life for all of us.

My earliest memories are of significant conflict between my parents, and often I served as the glue that kept them together. Dad was hard to please—often demanding and demeaning. Mom responded to him with manipulation to get what she wanted, making Dad feel guilty and withholding from him emotionally.

According to my parents, I was the best if not the only blessing in those early years of their marriage. But being that "blessing" brought overwhelming pressure. I was expected to model myself on my father, to be a small version of him. If I expressed a thought contrary to his, he belittled me for being stupid. If I didn't respond to a situation the way he wanted me to, he said I was weak. When I did something that earned his praise or affirmation, my success was turned around to make him look good.

When my parents fought, I often found myself in the middle. My mother took the role of innocent victim even when she provoked my father's wrath, and I would step in and divert his venom from her and onto me. Mom baited Dad into conflicts knowing I would become the whipping boy, which enabled her to comfort me while guilting Dad into feeling remorseful. That way she could appear to be the more loving parent. To this day that childhood dynamic plays out in my relationships: it is hard for me to receive comfort—from anyone—without suspecting that I'm being used in some way.

Six years after I was born, my sister joined the family. She was born with albinism, and all of us in the family responded by largely denying the limitations imposed by her condition. It was as if admitting that there was a problem would bring shame to the family. For example, although she was legally blind, she was permitted to get a driver's license. I also believe that my family's desire to encourage her to live and enjoy a fully functional life allowed me to question the reality of consequences. When I received a "no" answer from anyone, I responded in kind. Embedded within me was the belief that I didn't even need to heed such an answer. I believed there was always a way to get what I desired.

I learned early that the best way to deal with my father's demands, my mother's manipulation, and my sister's specialness was to work hard to be what each of them needed me to be. There were rewards, at times very unhealthy, for playing my role in the family. The intense verbal fights between my father and me, for example, rewarded me with the familiar sense of my place in the family. I'm sure that there were times that initiating a fight with my father was done knowing that mom would comfort me. Allowing her to do so not only was my way of getting back at dad, but also gave mom the gift of allowing her to continue her role of "victim" and "good parent." It was a vicious cycle that continues to some degree even today.

When I was in the sixth grade, my family moved to a different town. The transition was difficult, but it was made bearable by finding a good church. My new home brought my family face to face with a great fellowship of believers. I found in church the place where I could excel. Although I failed at making All-American as an athlete, I made the first string, so to speak, in the All-American church youth group team. My family basically lived at church. Church became my "being" because it met so many of my needs, not all of which were spiritual.

> **Church became my "being" because it met so many of my needs, not all of them spiritual.**

My success at church began to gain the approval of my father, for which I so desperately longed. I became "Mr. Youth Group" and accepted the responsibility of leadership. It was during this time that I felt led to a career in ministry.

This leadership responsibility allowed me to continue in the role of helper or fixer, but my personal life continued to be in desperate need. Being a church leader provided many years of approval from home and peers, but there were deep hurts and needs that I kept trying to fill with substitute behaviors, which haunted me and made my existence feel phony and fake.

In high school I did not try to hide that I was a "church boy"; the potential difficulties created by being a Christian and part of the 'in crowd' were compensated by my gift of being a people person and a people pleaser. At the Christian college I attended, I served in student leadership roles, traveled with student ministry groups, was heavily involved in the Baptist Student Union, and helped manage the intramural sports program. I flourished in the collegiate environment where I could continue to function in positions that helped me feel good about myself and also begin to fulfill my longings to be in the ministry. Although I took my desire to enter ministry seriously, and knew that I needed a good academic record to get a degree, I was much more interested in those social and ministry activities that gave me not only instant gratification, but also made me feel like I was either helping, doing, or fixing something.

My parents' marriage crumbled as I entered adulthood, and they divorced when I was in my late twenties. I remember vividly the day that I accepted the death of our family. I was in seminary, married, and my oldest child had just been born. Mom and Dad came for a visit, and when they left, I knew that their marriage was over. Nothing was said directly about them separating; I just knew through their interaction with each other during their visit that they had given up. The pain that surfaced that day is unlike any I have felt since. It seemed for the first time I had to accept that I couldn't fix it anymore. It was almost that somehow I had failed the family by not keeping us together.

My mother asked for my blessing on the divorce. With her discussion centering on how difficult it was to live with Dad's demanding and abusive behavior, I was unable to argue against her need for freedom. But it was not my blessing to give—I wasn't part of the decision to marry, and I wasn't the one who took those marriage vows—and now I regret agreeing to bless the dissolution of our family.

I married during my last year of college. I look back on those early years of marriage with great fondness. It was an exciting time for both of us, yet I do know that I wasn't the best husband. Many of the demanding behaviors modeled to me by my father began to surface. Things needed to go my own way, and when my wife opposed what I wanted, I became very angry and acted as if I was being mistreated. These traits made life difficult for my wife, yet she hung in there with me. It wasn't until my early thirties that I decided that I needed to resolve the unhealthy habit of pleasing people and start attending to my own needs.

I decided that I needed to resolve the unhealthy habit of pleasing people.

My first ministry position after college as a youth minister lasted only a short time, ending traumatically when I resigned for fear of being fired. I resigned when it became clear that I was not what the senior pastor thought I should be—a major wound for me. I was left without an identity because I was "called to be a minister." If I was deemed a failure in the ministry, then who was I? What was my purpose?

I survived and grew from that experience, but I kept the deep pain of that perceived failure to myself. I later went on to seminary and have had a successful career since. However, I need only to recall briefly that first experience to have all the pain well up within me.

Being a success in ministry initially came at a cost to my family and me. Being the consummate people pleaser meant that my nature led me to do or say whatever I needed to in order to keep everyone happy. I am good at discerning what others want from me, and I'd run myself ragged to achieve it. That also meant that I'd overwork, over commit, and never say "no," just to avoid conflict. If I needed to challenge someone and knew it would make that person unhappy, I'd choose to walk barefoot across hot coals instead. If something I'd done led to someone being unhappy with me, I'd do anything to make him or her happy with me. I constantly feared that one wrong move, for example upsetting the wrong person, would leave me unemployed.

I ran around the church jumping through hoops in order to keep everyone happy, or to be there for everyone, or to respond to everyone's crises, and my own family suffered. I would come home having spent my last bit of patience on others. I'd yell, demand, and belittle. I became my father.

Thank God that our nature can change. At the age of 34, twelve years into my professional career, I finally admitted that I needed to make major changes in my life. If I didn't, I feared that I would lose my ministry and my marriage and undoubtedly do irreparable damage to my two children. I was losing my ability to keep up the charade that I was happy and fulfilled. I also had to admit that I wasn't connected to God in the way I wanted and needed to be.

Dan's Reflection

John's story is shared here not because we expect all clergy to have experienced similar situations in their families of origin, but because we believe that many readers will relate to at least some points in John's experience. The purpose of his disclosure is to exemplify how our early experiences provide a natural setup for difficulties in later life. Alfred Adler, like Sigmund Freud, is known as a psychoanalytic theorist. Adler's major theoretical disagreement with classic Freudian beliefs centers on the belief that human beings are driven primarily by biological (sexual) and instinctual determination.[1] Adler did agree with Freud, however, that what a person becomes in adulthood is largely determined by the first five years of life.

Adler believed that people are motivated primarily by social urges, not sexual determinants. He proposed that life goals provide the source of human motivation, especially those goals that lead to security and that aid in overcoming feelings of inferiority.

It is this drive to compensate for the inferiority that we inherently possess that inspires us to move towards a sense of superiority. A person must compensate for this inferiority by seeking power—not power to dominate others or to be better than others, but rather power to move towards who she or he has the potential to become.

Adler believed that we create our *selves*, not that we are passively determined or shaped by experiences in childhood. It is not merely our childhood experiences that are crucial, but rather our attitude about these experiences that are critical. He also contended that the constellation of the family of origin often intensifies feelings of inferiority and leads to a faulty lifestyle.[2]

John's experience with his family fits into these basic tenets of Adler's theory. John made his entrance into the world at a difficult time in his parents' lives. Their relationship was fraught with difficulty, and John lived in a constantly tense environment from the beginning. He learned early that, in order to have some control over the chaos in his life, he needed to soothe the conflict in each of his parents. He became a people-pleaser and learned that, if he tried hard enough, he could make each of them happy by giving them what they wanted. As he grew and began to feel that he was unable to meet his father's expectations in the area of athletics, he developed and excelled in other areas that his father blessed, i.e., church, youth group, and music. This was a way for him to overcome feelings of inferiority.

As the "fixer" of the family, he often put himself in the middle of the chaos, hoping to alleviate it. He learned that if he could please his parents, then he had succeeded. If they gave him praise for his efforts, he felt loved. He believed that he had to work to earn love. Unconditional love was a foreign concept to him. He needed to find a way to compensate for his feeling of inferiority, and he did so by capitalizing on his success at church.

John's family-of-origin experience closely mirrors his ministry experience. The ministry was a good fit, because he was able to focus on the needs of others. When he did this, he felt better and therefore didn't need to worry about his own needs. Self-sacrifice is rewarded significantly in ministry circles.

When someone expressed gratitude for his help, let him know what a blessing he was or what a great job he'd done, then his identity and self-esteem soared. However, if people in the church were dissatisfied with his attempts or communicated that in some way he'd not met their expectations, then his identity became that of failure, and he fell into the depths of despair.

From his childhood and adolescence John took these beliefs about himself:

> ✠ If I am to be of value, I need to work at it.
> ✠ I am best at anticipating and meeting the needs of others.
> ✠ If I cannot make others happy, then I have failed.
> ✠ My value as a person comes from *what I do*, rather than *who I am*.

Family Issues and the Bible

In case you're wondering if there's any scriptural basis for these ideas surrounding family-of-origin issues, consider Numbers 14:18: "The LORD is slow to anger, abounding in love and forgiving sin and rebellion. Yet he does not leave the guilty unpunished; he punishes the children for the sin of the fathers to the third and fourth generation." At first glance, it sounds as if Moses is saying that if I sin, then my children, grandchildren, and great-grandchildren will be punished for my act. We don't believe that this is what Moses is communicating here.[3] Rather, Moses is stating that sinful behaviors are often passed down from generation to generation. As we have already noted, John learned certain behavioral patterns from his father, only to realize that he was living out his father's sins. Scripture clearly communicates truth; often the disastrous sins of a family are repeated for generations to come.

There are examples in the Bible of tragic results of a parent's behavior that are passed on to the children. David had an affair with Bathsheba, which resulted in a baby, who later died. David's children probably witnessed his manipulative behavior when he had Uriah killed in order to cover his sin with Bathsheba. This dysfunctional family became the environment in which David's son Amnon had an incestuous relationship with his half sister Tamar. Although David knew about this sin, he chose to deny its reality. It was never dealt with until Tamar's brother Absalom killed Amnon.

There are examples in the Bible of tragic results of a parent's behavior that are passed on to the children.

Dan's View: Seeking Professional Help

For some, addressing family-of-origin issues may be relatively easy. For others, it can be painful and complicated and may need to be done with the assistance of a professional counselor.

In my experience, ministry professionals as a whole are skeptical of therapy. Although I've had many church leaders make referrals to me—usually after reaching the limits of his or her counseling skills—most pastors are reluctant to enter counseling themselves.

Christians typically believe that once God is at the center of our lives, all emotional hurts are erased and we no longer suffer the results of them. While I believe that God has the power to remove both physical and emotional ailments instantaneously, He usually chooses to allow us to struggle through a healing process, often with the help of others.

The Bible also tells of God using others to aid in the healing process. A good example is found in the Gospel of John, chapter eleven. When Lazarus fell ill, his sisters, Mary and Martha, sent for Jesus because they knew that He could heal their brother. Four days after Lazarus was buried, Jesus arrived. Once He had comforted Mary and Martha, He approached Lazarus's tomb, and asked that the stone be removed.

"So they took away the stone. Then Jesus looked up and said, 'Father, I thank you that you have heard me.' . . . When He had said this, Jesus called in a loud voice, 'Lazarus, come out!'" (John 11:41,43).

The passage continues by saying that Lazarus, who had been dead, ". . . came forth, bound hand and foot with wrappings; and his face was wrapped around with a cloth" (v. 44). This place in the story is very significant. Even though Jesus was able to restore Lazarus to life, He chose not to use the same power to remove the death clothes that bound him. Instead, He loudly commanded Mary and Martha to "unbind him and set him free" (v. 44).

In the story of Lazarus we have a clear example of the counseling process. My role as a counselor is not to heal, but to unbind the death clothes holding one immobilized and blinded. "Death clothes" may include the impact that family-of-origin dysfunction has had on us.

Although we cannot do anything to change the past, the past significantly contributes to who we are today. When we examine our identity in terms of the past—our childhood—we run the risk of blaming other people and events on our current behavior. This is not healthy, nor is it what examining our family of origin entails.

John's examination of his family of origin was painfully difficult for him. Some may read his account and accuse him of blaming his parents and his upbringing for the problems in his life. But this is not about blame; it is about assigning correct cause. Fear of uncovering unpleasant truths can keep us from a healthy examination of the factors that have contributed to who we have become.

Common Obstacles

Here are typical excuses that keep us from taking an honest inventory of our life events.

The past is in the past. There's no reason to revisit what I can't change.

Although no one can argue that the past can't be changed, this excuse is invalid. If you tripped, fell, and broke your leg you probably wouldn't stand up, tell yourself that you broke your leg "in the past," and try to keep walking. Actually, denying the fact that it was broken and trying to walk on it anyway would undoubtedly cause additional damage.

"If I tell myself it doesn't hurt, then it won't" is the belief that leads to plenty of additional emotional damage. Unresolved emotional pain results in the need for medication to dull the pain. Medication such as drugs, sex, excessive materialism, and the need for increasing success and validation often assuage those in emotional pain. "Hard work" or an excessive absence of boundaries can also become a form of medication for this pain. Good works and the subsequent pats on the back prove to be adequate "Advil" for the troubled soul.

I am made new by God. Old things have passed.

Paul said, "Therefore, if anyone is in Christ, he is a new creation; the old has gone, the new has come!" (2 Cor 5:17). We have known many who use this quote to infer that once he or she is saved, this new life is free from the emotional damage done in the old life. As we read this Scripture, we find that Paul is referring to our spiritual selves, not the emotional or physical. If this were not so, then at the moment of our salvation our physical infirmities would also be instantaneously healed. What we can take from this verse is the guarantee that the sins that we have committed are no longer reckoned to us. We have been forgiven and made new by God.

The Bible says to honor my parents. That means
I can't find fault in what they did.

We believe the passages in Scripture that instruct us to honor our mother and father (Exod 20:12; Deut 5:16; Matt 15:4 and Eph 6:2) are often misunderstood. We have been told this means: never question or disagree with your parents, never hurt your parents, never put expectations on your parents, never tell your parents "no," and never do anything that would disappoint your parents. Supposedly these should be honored not only when you are a child, but also when you are an adult. This understanding is a serious misrepresentation of these instructions.

Careful examination of the word "honor" in these passages reveals that "to honor" means to "give weight to." In essence, if you "give weight to" your parents, then their impact on you will be significant. For example, when parents are loving, nurturing, and giving, one honors them by allowing their love, nurture, and gifts to have a weighted impact. By the same token, when parents do damage (either intentionally or unintentionally), if one honors them, the negative impact will have a weighted effect.

Acknowledging that our parents have hurt us by their actions, but not being disrespectful, is in fact giving honor to them. It is not honoring to pretend that our parents were perfect when they weren't. Honoring your mother and father does not mean you are to give them a free pass to escape responsibility for his and her behavior.

It is not honoring to pretend that our parents were perfect when they weren't.

There are those in therapy (children and adults) whose parents hid behind the mistaken belief that being honored by their children meant that they were exempt from responsibility for their harmful, dysfunctional behavior. It is honoring at its best when we are honest about the dysfunction we experienced in our family of origin. It allows everyone involved to address hurts, experience forgiveness, and make changes for the future.

I don't need professional help; I have God.

Naaman was General of the Army under the king of Aram. He was held in high esteem by the king, and although Naaman was revered for his greatness, this mighty man of valor suffered with leprosy. A captured girl, the servant to Naaman's wife, appeared happy in her captivity and from a genuine care for Naaman said to his wife, "'If only my master would see the prophet who is in Samaria! He would cure him of his leprosy.' Naaman went to his master and told him what the girl from Israel had said. 'By all means, go,' the king of Aram replied. 'I will send a letter to the king of Israel.' . . . The letter that he took to the king of Israel read: 'With this letter I am sending my servant Naaman to you so that you may cure him of his leprosy'" (2 Kgs 5:3-6).

The passage continues to tell that, when the King of Israel read the letter, he became very angry that he was put in the position of God to instantaneously make Naaman well. The prophet Elisha heard of his anger, and sent word to the King to send Naaman to him.

Naaman showed up at the house of Elisha, but waited at the door because he was too proud to enter the humble house. Elisha sent instructions through a messenger that Naaman was to wash himself seven times in the muddy, grimy Jordan River so that he would be healed of his affliction.

Naaman was enraged, and ". . . went away angry and said, 'I thought that he would surely come out to me and stand and call on the name of the LORD his God, wave his hand over the spot and cure me of my leprosy. Are not Abana and Pharapar, the rivers of Damascus, better than any of the waters of Israel? Couldn't I wash in them and be cleansed? So he turned and went off in a rage" (2 Kgs 5:11-12).

Were it not for his servants who implored him to do what he was told, Naaman would have never been healed. Verse 14 says, ". . . he went down and dipped himself in the Jordan seven times, as the man of God had told him, and his flesh was restored and became clean like that of a young boy."

In my (Dan's) work with clients the essence of this story is relevant, especially among Christians. We tend to believe that God will instantaneously heal us. It is not often that we want to revisit painful memories or address the ugliness of our behaviors that lead to unhealthy living. Quite often, therapy is an unpleasant experience that we wish to avoid, much like Naaman who thought surely there was cleaner water elsewhere that would achieve the same results as the muddy Jordan.

I've had many clients leave therapy because they don't want to do the difficult work necessary for healing. Thankfully, many of them return later when they are ready to address issues. Sadly, not all of them do.

Several years ago, I worked very briefly in therapy with a young man who had suffered a great deal in his adolescence. His parents were not only negligent, but also very physically and emotionally abusive. A short time after he entered therapy, he gave his life to God. I believe his conversion experience was sincere, and was responsible for his changed perspective of life.

This young man became part of a church that did not support the notion of psychotherapy. In fact, his pastor told him it was not what God wanted for him, and that God would heal him if he lived a righteous life. Eventually, this young man left therapy confident in the fact that, because God was at the center of his life, He would take away all the problems he had struggled with his whole adult life. I never heard from him again, but found out that less than six months after leaving therapy he committed suicide.

> **Salvation and a righteous life do not eliminate the need for attention to our human condition.**

It is erroneous to believe that salvation and living a righteous life eliminates the need for attention to our human condition. It's no different than saying that our need for air, water, food, and medical attention is eliminated once we've accepted Christ. As we discussed earlier, 2 Corinthians 5:17 promises that God will make us new; this verse does not promise to erase the effects of the life we lived before we came to Christ.

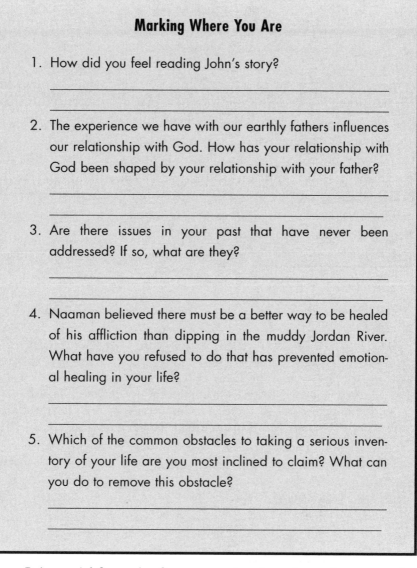

Marking Where You Are

1. How did you feel reading John's story?

2. The experience we have with our earthly fathers influences our relationship with God. How has your relationship with God been shaped by your relationship with your father?

3. Are there issues in your past that have never been addressed? If so, what are they?

4. Naaman believed there must be a better way to be healed of his affliction than dipping in the muddy Jordan River. What have you refused to do that has prevented emotional healing in your life?

5. Which of the common obstacles to taking a serious inventory of your life are you most inclined to claim? What can you do to remove this obstacle?

It is crucial for each of us to examine those issues in our past in order to identify the faulty or unhealthy traits that impact our functioning. This will require some to enlist the help of a professional counselor, an experience that may require him or her to ignore biases and misconceptions perpetuated in some Christian circles.

The First Mark

So, how does addressing these issues help someone to carry out his or her ministry? A keen awareness of our tendencies always helps to ensure that we're acting from correct motives. Usually, our natural proclivities come from those factors in our formation that had the heaviest impact. When we have taken the time to wrestle with these tendencies, we can begin to act as Christ calls us to act. Our family upbringing, our childhood experiences are no longer detriments to our ministries. God transforms us and our ministries, bringing about change and wholeness. *The first mark of a healthy ministry professional is that he or she has addressed and resolved issues that relate to his or her family of origin.*

Chapter One References

[1] Gerald Corey, *Theory and Practice of Psychotherapy*, 2nd ed. (Belmont, CA: Brooks/Cole, 1982).

[2] Ibid.

[3] Consider the words of Ezekiel 18:14-18 which says, "But suppose this son has a son who sees the sins his father commits, and though he sees them, he does not do such things. . . . He will not die for his father's sin; he will surely live. But his father will die for his own sin, because he practiced extortion, robbed his brother and did what was wrong among his people."

A Distorted View of "Call"

Many people mistake our work for our vocation.
Our vocation is the love of Jesus.
Mother Theresa

You did not choose me, but I chose you and appointed you
to go and bear fruit—fruit that will last *(John 15:16)*.

What "Call" Is

In this chapter we look at what it means to be "called" by God. Through this discovery, we encourage you to examine your own call. In so doing, you will be able to separate the healthy from the unhealthy with the purpose of refining your call.

What exactly is a call? We are all familiar with biblical call: Abram, Moses, Noah, Isaiah, Jonah, and Paul. An initial answer to that question would most likely be that a call results in action. God said, "Go," and they went. God said, "Do," and they did. A major premise of the book is that as we grow in relationship with God, we move away from "doing" towards "being." Does this also apply to being called? In other words, are we called to *do* something or to *be* something?

> **As we grow in relationship with God, we move away from "doing" towards "being."**

Historically, Christianity has used the word "call" to describe one's conviction of being chosen by God to serve Him. However, we believe that when God places a call on a person's life, He is calling that person into a relationship with Him. When we choose to heed this call and cultivate an intimate relationship, His leading will become apparent in all areas of life. Our passions, desires, gifts, and talents given by God move us in the direction He has for us. This includes, but is not limited to, things such as education, vocation, who to marry, and what ministries to support financially.

A Call to Ministry

I (John) associate the word "call" with the sense of hearing. A dial tone, push-button beeps, a ring, and a person's voice on the other line are what I think of when envisioning a "call."

My call into the ministry was not at all an audible message. If I were to most describe it, I would refer to it more as a *feeling*. It was more of something I *sensed* rather than what I *heard*. I felt an overwhelming presence of God encouraging me to do something special with my life for Him. Back then, I believed that to be called of God meant only one thing, to go into full time ministry. So that's what I did.

I must admit that my perception of "call" has changed, as has my attitude and my commitment. Let me describe the evolution of my call. As I've previously mentioned, from the sixth grade onward, church was very important to me. I attended everything possible on both Sundays and Wednesdays; if the church doors were open, I was there. My youth group's focus centered on its youth choir. This choir was not only very challenging to me, but also provided a sense of fun and accomplishment that I did not find anywhere else. Our youth group took music and choir very seriously, and it was amazing what God, through our director, did with about thirty-five average kids.

My first choir director was a fellow by the name of Bobby Jones. During that time of my needy adolescence, Bobby became my hero. He had the ability to balance the seriousness of a moment, such as the need to practice, with fun, like when someone croaked or came in at the wrong time.

Bobby also had the ability to live life the same way. He integrated the seriousness of living a relationship with Christ while living out the fun things in life. He helped me to explore my interest in music, and introduced me to the writings of Grady Nutt, a Christian comedian, which had a significant impact on me as a young Christian. He taught me that working for God (in the church) could be a good thing. Most importantly he helped me to see that spiritual things really came from within, and that the outside things were really not important. For young people, church is easily a drag, but Bobby helped us all find place and meaning in the institutional church.

I was devastated during my sophomore year of high school; Bobby left our church to pursue his doctoral degree in music. I realized my gratitude to have had the opportunity to be impacted by a great leader.

After Bobby left, I began to wonder if God could use me in such a mighty way and decided that, through His power, He could. I publicly acknowledged my "call" to full time Christian service during my sophomore year of high school.

As I revisit that period of my life, I am somewhat skeptical of the process leading to my call. I do believe that God wants me to be in the ministry, and I believe that God has blessed my ministry as I've honored my commitment to Him. However, my desire to pursue the ministry came from a gratitude for Bobby. Simply put, I wanted to follow in his footsteps, and I wanted to have an impact on someone just as he impacted me. Though my motives were probably unhealthy, God honored my heart in this matter. Hero worship is not a healthy reason to pursue the ministry. Clearly, this is an example of how God can take something unhealthy and use it for something good.

Immediately upon making my call public, I received praise, accolades, and kudos for my decision. I was thrilled to be chosen as the student pastor on youth Sunday "because of my call." Also, as a "result of my call," I was elected to be president of the youth choir. "Because I was called" I was asked to serve on committees and represent the youth in important matters of the church. My ego grew with these special considerations. Announcing my call to the ministry had elevated me to a higher social class in the church.

This special treatment did provide direction, which I needed. At the same time it provided much personal pain and anguish. My elevated status provided by others also came with the belief that I was now different, or at least should be. It was as if this call made me "perfect," and I was expected to rise above the struggles of my peers. Those years were difficult for me. I struggled with issues and sinned just as my peers did. I faced a dilemma. If I was truly special and "perfect" as those around me seemed to believe, then how could I struggle with unhealthy behaviors? My struggles with sin led me to feel very insincere, phony, and downright dirty. My desires to serve God and to grow to be more Christlike were real, yet I felt that one day I would be discovered as a fraud.

As I progressed in my career, the looming fear that "John will be discovered as a fake" threatened my inner life. I needed to cope with my inconsistencies. Instead of viewing my call as a blessing, I saw it as my job. Ministry then became more about *what I did,* rather than a result of *who I was.*

My "call" eventually manifested itself in merely fulfilling the duties of a job. My energies were spent keeping things afloat and keeping people happy. I was unaware that I was called to the ministry because God called me to Him and had infused me with specific gifts, talents, and personality. I did not know that these gifts mixed with the flaws of my humanness, that made me what He wanted me to be, so that I might impact His Kingdom.

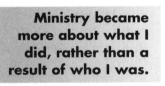

Ministry became more about what I did, rather than a result of who I was.

Was it simply that God called me to be the associate pastor of First Baptist Church and to take on the tasks and ministries that the job entails? Or did he call me to be John Daniels in all of my flawed completeness, so that I might have the earthly role of professional minister? Calling is not about taking on a role that completes a task. It is about fulfillment of personhood and relationship with my Maker.

A Story of True Calling

David Dunn is a pretty ordinary man. In his forties, he lives a rather lackluster life in Philadelphia with his wife Audrey and his son Joseph. He performs the mundane duties of a security guard at a football stadium. Though he had been a star football player in college, David brought his athletic career to an end after he and his then-girlfriend, 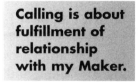 Audrey, survived a serious car accident. While he was unscathed, he pretended to have been hurt in the accident. He did so to remain in relationship with Audrey, knowing she would never marry a football player.

Now, many years later, this deception has taken its toll on his marriage relationship; he and his wife are emotionally estranged. David plods through life with a deep sense of sadness. He is unfulfilled in his job, and he lives with the knowledge that he ended his football career under false pretenses. While he is on a trip home from a job interview in New York, the train derails. David survives the train wreck, the sole survivor of 132 passengers, and after the train wreck he meets a man named Elijah Price. Elijah, an art dealer specializing in comic book drawings, begins to instruct David on the nature of heroes and their powers. Slowly, through his relationship with Elijah, the pieces of his life begin to come together.

Both David and Elijah are fictional characters in M. Night Shyamalan's movie *Unbreakable*. This modern-day tale of superhero and nemesis reveals that the dark sadness under which David functions every day of his life is due to his denial of his true call. Slowly he begins to accept that he is unbreakable. He also comes to realize that he possesses the ability to see evil and the physical strength to protect people.

His denial slowly fades as two people in his life—Elijah, who is later revealed as David's archenemy, and Joseph, David's son—consistently show David the truth about himself.

The most poignant scene in the movie is the morning after David saves two children held hostage by a man who killed their parents. David reveals to Joseph that by saving the children, he has accepted his calling. He knows who he is. At the close of the movie, Elijah asks him a question: "When you woke this morning, was it still there? The sadness?" David answers with a sobering, "No."

We use this vignette to illustrate true calling. David's purpose was beyond that of a star football player and even that of a security guard. Because he refused to look beyond his occupation, he felt purposeless and empty. Accepting his call, who he truly was, did not change the external features of David's life. However, accepting his calling and living it from his inner being brought him a sense of peace. The change was intensely personal, not even visible to most of those around him.

So it is with all of us. Knowing and accepting our call provides peace. We often confuse call with what we do, rather than who we are. We spin our wheels in an attempt to do, do, do—hoping to make a difference. We refuse to acknowledge the truth of the words that Elijah speaks to Audrey, "It's hard for many to believe there are extraordinary things inside themselves. . . ." Sadly, ministry leaders get caught up in the "doing" part of their ministry; usually at the expense of the true call on his or her life.

> **Ministry leaders get caught up in the "doing" part at the expense of their true call.**

Biblical Accounts of Being Called

Through Scripture's accounts of those called by God, we are able to form a picture of "call."

Paul realizes that acceptance of call is not evidenced by works, but rather through a connection with God.

In Romans 3 and 4 Paul talks about works (doing). He uses Abraham as an example. Basically, Paul says, "If there was ever anyone who could boast or be justified by good deeds and works, it was Abraham" (Rom 4:1). However, in Romans 4:13 he says, "It was not through the law that Abraham and his offspring received the promise that he would be the heir of the world, but through the righteousness that comes by faith." What does this mean? Simply, Abraham's calling or justification came because of his faith—his *being* not his *doing*.

Though there is room for debate about "call," it is clear to us through Scripture that we are called to one thing only. We are called into relationship with God through Christ.

Jesus prayed, "Now this is eternal life: that they know you, the only true God, and Jesus Christ, whom you have sent" (John 17:3). Philippians 3:10 states, "I want to know Christ and the power of his resurrection and the fellowship of sharing in his sufferings." Henry Blackaby and Kerry Skinner say in their book *Called and Accountable*: "The call to salvation is at the same time a call to be redemptively on mission with God in our world." Blackaby goes on to say, "For many the greatest challenge is not that they do not know the will of God, but rather that they do know this will but have not been willing to be obedient to Him!"

So what does this mean in light of defining "call"? Our highest calling is to relationship with God, not to vocation or activity. Through that relationship we are filled with His spirit in order to accomplish His purposes and ways. Not only a select few are to be "on mission" for God, but all of us are. Great debate could be made over the calling of clergy and the unique nature of that call. However, we believe that all are called to be on mission for God. The belief that a calling into full-time Christian ministry is a greater call than any other profession is a fallacy and often sets up a person in a ministry profession for failure. We'll discuss this in more detail later.

When David returns to God, it is through relationship.

"Blessed is the man who does not walk in the council of the wicked or stand in the way of sinners, or sit in the seat of mockers. But his delight is in the law of the LORD and on his law he meditates day and night. He is like a tree planted by streams of water, which yields its fruit in season and whose leaf does not wither. Whatever he does prospers" (Ps 1:1-3).

It is hard to imagine that the author of this wonderful Psalm is an adulterer and murderer. Where did David go wrong? The Scriptures say that when he was confronted by Nathan after the death of his child, "David got up from the ground. After he had washed, put on lotions and changed his clothes, he went into the house of the

LORD and worshiped" (2 Sam 12:20). Can you imagine? He went to be with the Lord and worshiped. We must remember that in the Old Testament worship was being in the presence of the Lord. Basically, David learned the lesson that what was wrong in his life was more than the act of sin. It was the lack of relationship with the Lord. David could have built a new temple or offered multiple sacrifices to signify his return to God. However, his return was marked by the restoration of relationship. He communed with God.

Peter learns the cost of relationship with Jesus.

John 13:37-38 says, "Peter asked, 'Lord, why can't I follow you now? I will lay down my life for you.' Then Jesus answered, 'Will you really lay down your life for me? I tell you the truth, before the rooster crows, you will disown me three times.'"

Jesus is challenging Peter regarding his true relationship with Him. Jesus was not suggesting that Peter was unfit, or that he could not do the right things; he challenged the relationship—the "being" not the "doing." In essence, Jesus was saying, "I know, Peter, that

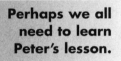
Perhaps we all need to learn Peter's lesson.

you are loyal, strong, and committed. But when it comes down to it, you will value your own life more than your relationship with me." Peter needed to learn this lesson, and perhaps we all do. In John 21 we read about the reinstatement of Peter. Notice the question from Jesus, "Do you love me?" This was a relationship challenge. Jesus wants Peter to "be" before he "does"—"If you love me (being), then feed my sheep (do)."

God acknowledges relationship with us before we are capable of doing.

Jeremiah 1:4-5 says, "The word of the LORD came to me, saying, 'Before I formed you in the womb, I *knew* you [relationship], before you were born I set you apart; I appointed you as a prophet to the nations.'" What were the qualifications for Jeremiah's call? Was it training, physical abilities, heredity? No, it was relationship. "I knew you." Holy Scripture gives us great insight into calling in these verses. First, God is in control. Second, God chooses us before we choose him. Third, relationship is mandatory. Fourth, power for action comes from God.

Verse six continues, "'Ah, Sovereign LORD . . . I do not know how to speak; I am only a child.' But the LORD said to me, 'Do not say, "I am only a child." You must go to everyone I send you to and say whatever I command you. Do not be afraid of them. for I am with you and will rescue you,' declares the LORD."

People of the Old Testament lived under the law. The law was all about doing the right thing. Living under the law did not require relationship or intimacy (though some practiced it). It simply required *doing* the law, staying out of trouble, and checking the "done" box on a giant to-do list. In the New Testament, Jesus came so that we could have *relationship* with God (John 15:1-4).

> **It is not that we should stop doing, but that doing should come out of relationship.**

Relationship with God was possible through Jesus. The mode of doing has been replaced by being (relationship). This is not to imply that we should stop doing, but rather, doing should come out of relationship with Jesus. We give to the poor because we love Christ. We love others because Christ first loved us. We love our neighbor because we want to show him or her the love of God.

Mary and Martha: being vs. doing

Probably the most classic example of Jesus' distinguishing between "being" and "doing" is when He is visiting Mary and Martha. "As Jesus and his disciples were on their way, he came to a village where a woman named Martha opened her home to him. She had a sister called Mary, who sat at the Lord's feet listening to what he said. But Martha was distracted by all the preparations that had to be made. She came to him and asked, 'Lord, don't you care that my sister has left me to do the work by myself? Tell her to help me!' 'Martha, Martha,' the Lord answered, 'you are worried and upset about many things, but only one thing is needed. Mary has chosen what is better, and it will not be taken away from her.'"

"It will not be taken away from her." We should apply this powerful statement to our lives. As ministry professionals we have come to believe that our call is to works, such as serving in the church, on the mission field, and so on. We know numerous pastors that claim 1 Corinthians 9:16 as their mantra/mission statement or life verse:

". . . for I am compelled to preach. Woe to me if I do not preach the gospel!" For these, the role of pastor or preacher is their identity. Losing the forum to "be the pastor" would leave them without an identity. The venue in which we serve God can change. We can lose our job, or even lose the ability to function in our job. Would this mean that call is lost? Do we cease to function out of our purpose if we are no longer in a Christian vocation?

What "Call" Is Not

Here are some common myths about being called to ministry.

Myth #1: Call is to vocation.

As stated previously, we hold to the biblical belief that, when God calls us, it is an invitation to enter a relationship with Him. It is a myth to believe that God calls us into a job, career, or vocation. Obviously, when we are in one accord with God, He will direct all elements of our lives, and this will include the vocation we enter. However, nowhere in Scripture do we find that God called anyone into his or her vocation. Without question, there are biblical examples of those who *fulfill* his or her call by accomplishing specific tasks for God: David as king, Moses as liberator, and Joshua as commander of Israel's armies.

> **Heeding the call to relationship with Him allows divine orchestration of our lives.**

We maintain that to be called of God is to be called into relationship with Him. Heeding this call and deepening a relationship with Him allows divine orchestration of all components of our life including the development of our gifts, talents, and interests that lead to our vocation.

To believe that a "call" to serve God is heard in terms of vocation makes us vulnerable to believing Myth #2.

Myth #2: Career Christian service is the highest calling.

We actually found it in writing! In *God's Call: The Cornerstone of Effective Ministry* the authors actually put into writing—what we believe to be—one of the most dangerous myths that lead clergy to personal destruction and professional burnout.

As one called by God to vocational ministry, you have been anointed by him for this role. God has placed His hand on your life and has set you aside for His service. This is a very special calling—the highest (p. 21).

. . . You may ask, "Why is it so important for people to sense that they are called by God to vocational ministry?" This is an important question. If ministry were a business or other profession, it wouldn't matter. You could be a leader in any area through education and experience. You could develop the necessary skills to perform your assigned tasks. But vocational ministry is different. This work has a supernatural element. It cannot be done by just anyone; it must be done by those who are called and anointed by God (p. 20).[1]

There is grave danger in believing and perpetuating the belief that one who is "called to the ministry" is somehow more special than someone who is led to another career. Based upon what we said previously, a "call" is into relationship with God. The danger in believing that a career in ministry is greater than any other is twofold. First, it has the potential to set the individual apart in such a way that she eventually comes to believe that she functions under a different set of expectations than others (these dangers are explained in more detail later). Secondly it leads those in other professions to believe that they are less a part of the kingdom if their life's work is spent doing something other than traditional ministry.

There is grave danger in the belief that one "called to the ministry" is somehow more special.

God's Call tells this story: Al was married with two children, working at a hospital and serving God as a lay member of his church when a friend asked him when he was going to give up his job and go to work for God. That night he prayed and asked God if He really did want him to preach. Like Gideon, Al asked God for a sign. "Lord, if You want me to preach, then ring a bell!" As Al and his family drove to church the next Wednesday night, the air conditioner on the car broke and the windows were rolled down. Out of nowhere a herd of cows blocked the road, and right in the middle of that herd was one big cow with a bell tied around her neck. That bell was ringing for Al! He said, "Yes, Lord, I'll preach!"

A man who is working in a hospital and a lay member of his church may very well be doing the will of God. Yes, it may have been God's directing that led this man from his hospital work to become a minister. The point we want to illuminate is that work in a professional capacity as "minister" has no greater eternal, kingdom value than working in any other profession.

The authors continue with another story of an associate pastor who worked in a "secular job" for seventeen years prior to "going into the ministry." Upon quitting his job and attending seminary "His prayer now is to live a long life and give God back the 6,000 days it took him to answer the special call of God on his life." The sad news is you can't get back any day that has passed. He wrongly assumes that those 6,000 days had been wasted because he wasn't working in a church. If all of us who truly seek God were to go into the pastorate, the world would be in trouble.

We run the risk of sounding harsh as we attempt to burst this bubble. The truth remains: you are not special simply because you've been to seminary, have a church to lead, are a great orator, have people clamoring to have you marry their children, say a splendid prayer over dinner when you're invited to their home for a meal, visit them in the hospital, or bury them when they're dead and gone.

What makes you special is that you have been handcrafted by your heavenly Father to fulfill His purpose for your life—whatever be that purpose. Seeking intimacy with God, living life that is pleasing to Him, and finding value in your place in His life is what makes you a worthy and productive servant for Him.

> **Intimacy with God, a life pleasing to Him, and finding value in your own place, all make you a worthy and productive servant.**

Myth #3 Never question nor doubt your call.

The author of *God's Call* talks about a time in his own career when he doubted his call.

> . . . one way Satan [tries] to stop us from impacting our world through vocational ministry is to cause us to doubt our call. If he can confuse us, we will pursue other things with our lives. When I was in college, I experienced a time when I began to doubt my

call to the ministry. I was uncertain about what I was to do. I was troubled because all the people back in the church where I grew up would be disappointed. The church had helped me financially with my education. I was confused and didn't want to face the issue because of the embarrassment it might cause. Finally, I had to deal with it and get it settled.

A revival team I was a part of had a meeting scheduled a week away. I apologized to God about needing a visible sign that the ministry was where I should invest my life. I asked God to have at least one person come forward during the five days of the revival. I didn't tell anyone about the doubt I was experiencing because it was so personal and important to me. When the revival began I was nervous because of what was at stake for me. No one came forward the first service, second service, third or fourth. After the fourth service, I got away by myself and simply poured out my heart before God. I explained that I wanted to know His will for my life and that it appeared I had misread what He had for me. I asked for help in getting through the last service and promised Him I never would preach again after that service if no one came forward. I had settled it and was ready to swallow my pride if it was clear that the ministry wasn't God's will for me.[2]

This young man made it all the way to "near the end of the last stanza" of the invitation hymn before two women came forward. Our hearts go out to this young man who desperately wanted to please his heavenly Father, but held his breath throughout the entire song hoping for a "sign" that would assure him of his value in God's eyes. It's as if he believed in order to be useful to God and the kingdom, he had to have a career in the ministry.

He concludes this story with, "I thanked God for showing me His will and apologized for such a glaring lack of faith. I needed something visible and God provided. The next day back at college, I received word that 29 other people made decisions in the evening service as a direct result of the revival. I had my answer, and I had it clearly. This was where God wanted me to invest my life. Vocational ministry was God's clear plan for me."

We want to be very careful here, as we have no right to question this man's motives or call. We don't know him, and we don't know what he's done for God since this event. However, we have several concerns with his story and disagree with some of his conclusions.

First, doubting or questioning one's call to the ministry, or any profession for that matter, is not necessarily from Satan. Too many people have walked the aisle in a moment of emotion and declared their "call to preach." It is possible for any one of us to claim this, when it is not actually God's plan for us.

> **We encourage anyone entering the ministry to question and examine his or her call.**

We encourage, if not implore, anyone entering the ministry to question and examine his or her call.

Second, if we were sitting with this young man and heard his account, we would have to question if he was really searching for God's call, or if he was pleading with God to allow him to have his own way because he wanted so badly to be in vocational ministry. By his own admission, he was afraid of what the folks at home would say if he admitted that he wasn't called to the ministry. He didn't want to be embarrassed.

We don't know why those women didn't respond until the fifth and final night of the revival, and we don't know how many verses of "Just as I Am" were sung before these two women walked the aisle. It was as if this young man was telling God, "I want to be of value to you, so I must be called to be a pastor; *please*, let me be a pastor."

Myth #4: A call to ministry will result in personal reward.

This myth seems to be pervasive among clergy and is also a predominant thought among Christians in general. But our commitment to God and our service to Him should have *nothing* to do with what we get out of it. Worshiping God should never be about us, but solely about Him. How many times do we get in the way of God's work because we want to feel good about what we're doing?

The need for this type of affirmation seems unbiblical to us. We are not promised assurance. We are certainly not promised that we will see the fruit of our efforts. We should not pursue any undertaking for the sake of self-satisfaction. We should not seek affirmation from men; we should only be motivated by simple faith and obedience and find purpose only in our relationship with Him.

Pastors on the brink of burnout often say things like, "I just want to know that I make a difference." "I just want to see the fruit of my labor." "I just want to know that people care and will respond to God." While it is human nature to need to feel productive, nowhere in the Scriptures do we find that we will ever see the results of our efforts for the Kingdom.

Several years ago Ray Boltz wrote and popularized a song entitled "Thank You."[3] The message of this song is told through one who dreamed that he went to heaven. In the dream he encounters several people who thank him for his part in their conversion—essentially, were it not for him they would not be in heaven. The chorus:

> Thank you for giving to the Lord.
> I am a life that was changed.
> Thank you for giving to the Lord.
> I am so glad you gave.

While the song itself could encourage Christians to make efforts to lead the lost to Christ, should others' gratitude be our reason to evangelize? In Revelation 22:8 John states, "I, John, am the one who heard and saw these things. And when I had heard and seen them, I fell down to worship at the feet of the angels who had been showing them to me. But he said to me, 'Do not do it! I am a fellow servant with you and with your brothers the prophets and of all who keep the words of this book. Worship God!'" We fear that it's almost blasphemous to insinuate that when we get to heaven people will be praising us. All of our energy for all of eternity will be spent praising and worshiping God—it will not be about us! Unfortunately, the popular Christian movement seems to support the notion that it's all about what we get from it.

Cutting through the Myths

Several years ago I (Dan) went on a mission trip to a Central American country. Many, if not most, of the people on this mission trip were veterans of past trips, some having been to this same country, city, and specific population numerous times.

We were there a week, and we worked very hard at our planned task. We slept very little and came back exhausted. I was troubled by what I heard over and over from several of the trip's veterans, "It's worth the hard work and effort to come here because, unlike people at home, these people are so thankful for what we do."

I am deeply troubled by an attitude that communicates that the reason we do things for God is because it gives *us* something, or makes *us* feel good. We have become people who need to be rewarded in some way in order to give to others. Most conflicts in the church today over such issues as worship style come from this same concept: If I don't hear the kind of music I like, if the pastor steps on my toes or raises the bar and it makes me uncomfortable, then I need to find another church." How many times have you heard someone who is leaving the church state the reason, ". . . because I'm not being fed"?

I want to share some of my own experience in regard to being "called." About the same time that John realized that he was to enter the ministry as a profession, I was about to graduate from high school. I clearly remember the day the graduating class of 1979 stood before the congregation of North Baptist Church each declaring our plans for our futures. I was planning to attend college to major in social work. My girl friend—who is now my wife—planned to attend college to become a registered nurse. Although we were showered with support from the congregation, we did not receive the same blessing as those who were planning to "enter the ministry."

In the years since, I have been at several different churches, and graduation Sundays replay the same scenario. Those entering Bible colleges or those declaring their "calling into the ministry" have been given special scholarships, speaking opportunities when home for vacations, and unique prayers of blessing.

I suppose the recollection of my graduation experience is marked by recollections of jealousy and feeling left out. However, as I've matured, I've come to realize that the message of their "unique" calling as they headed off to Bible school was not accurate, and perhaps it even set them up for unfortunate expectations.

As previously stated, nowhere in Scripture does it speak of any "calling" being greater than another. First Corinthians 12:14-31 says, "Now the body is not made up of one part but many. If the foot should say, 'Because I am not a hand, I do not belong to the body,' it would not for that reason cease to be part of the

> **Nowhere in Scripture does it speak of any calling being greater than another.**

body. . . . On the contrary, those parts of the body that seem to be weaker are indispensable, and the parts that we think are less honorable we treat with special honor. . . . God has combined the members of the body and has given greater honor to the parts that lacked it. So that there should be no division in the body, but that its parts should have equal concern for each other." This passage of Scripture clearly makes the point that there is none better than another—that no gift is greater than another. And most importantly, there is no "calling" greater than another.

The reason that I write this with so much passion is that I have been a firsthand witness not only to the personal destruction of those under the spiritual authority of a minister with this belief, but I have also counseled ministry professionals who themselves have been damaged by belief of this myth.

Several years ago I was counseling the teenage son of a prominent pastor. During the months I met with this young man, he spoke often of witnessing his father beat his mother. In a family session, the father admitted to me that he did regularly physically abuse his wife, and he was justified by his action because she was not submissive enough to him. Eventually, his wife filed for divorce, and I was subpoenaed to court to testify to his admission of spousal abuse. In the days leading to my court appearance, I received numerous threatening letters and phone calls from members of his congregation promising the wrath of God should I sully the reputation of their pastor. I even received a letter from the pastor himself, who through the abuse of Scripture, warned me of certain destruction. He quoted: "Who can lay a hand on the Lord's anointed and be guiltless?" (1 Sam 26:9) and, "Do not touch my anointed one; do my prophets no harm" (1 Chr 16:22).

Somewhere in his spiritual development and call to ministry this "man of God" came to believe that he was above reproach. He not only believed that God wouldn't have a problem with his beating his wife into submission while his children huddled together in fear, but also that he could use Scripture to keep someone from shining the light on his atrocity.

I have counseled many clergy who have found themselves in the dark pit of sinful living, yet they still functioned in their roles on Sunday. Sexual affairs with church members, frequenting prostitutes, using church money for personal reasons, hidden drug and alcohol addictions, and child pornography have all been confessed to me in my counseling office. Surprising numbers of these men shamefully admitted that they permitted themselves to enter into such activities because they somehow felt justified *because they were pastors!*

Regarding the Ray Boltz song, I'm going to go out on a limb. I do not believe that God cares whether or not we are fulfilled and feel good about what we do for Him. I do not claim to be a theologian, but I believe He wants us to put our "nose to the grindstone" and, out of obedience, do what He expects of us.

"After all I've done for so-and-so, and this is how he treats me." I've heard this statement often from pastors who are struggling with feelings of fruitlessness. Underneath this statement is the belief that, "If I help people, they should be appreciative of me and give me something in return." Where is this concept found in Scripture? Nowhere.

> **I believe He wants us to put our "nose to the grindstone" and do what He expects of us.**

Calling It Like It Is

Flipping through TV channels recently, I (John) happened upon a telecast of a large church's service. The pastor was preaching about the favor of God, and how great it is to experience the favor of God. To illustrate this, he recounted an experience he had in an airport. He was thinking about the favor of God as he walked to the gate of his next plane's departure. After giving his boarding pass to the agent, he was told that there was a mix-up with seating, and as a result he would be bumped into first class. He went on to describe the comfortable seats, the exquisite food, and how he was treated like royalty, which he attributed to the favor of God. He said, "My God is so good, and you can experience God's favor too, if you just have enough faith!" I was dumbfounded as I thought about the seventy-year-old lady who perhaps sat at the back of the plane. Was she out of the favor of God?

The Bible never speaks of an easy life if we follow God. It speaks of no rewards on earth if we follow God. In fact, it warns of persecution if we fol-

> **The Bible never speaks of an easy life if we follow God.**

low God. It is dangerous for those of us who serve God—professionally or otherwise—to expect that we will feel rewarded for our kingdom efforts.

The Second Mark

John S. Powers in his article entitled "Surviving the Pastorate" (lifeway.com/pastor) lists four misconceptions often held by pastors. They are:

① *If I am called of God, then they will follow.* That's no guarantee. Moses was called of God, and the children of Israel resisted him every step of the wilderness way. Just because we are called of God doesn't mean our people will always follow us.

② *If I do the "right things," then I will avoid problems.* No chance! Would you agree that the Apostle Paul did the right things? Problems come with the territory!

③ *If I leave where I am serving, the next place will be better.* Honestly, probably not. Remember, your "green field" was someone else's "brown field." Leaving a church for another church is not always the answer.

④ *If I go to a larger church, I will not face problems.* Larger churches have more people and greater opportunities. It's true. But with more people come larger quantitative and qualitative problems. That means a minister of a larger church than yours has more problems and deeper problems than you face in your present church setting. Don't believe a large church guarantees an easy path.

These misconceptions seem to have at their root the issue of feeling good about the work we do for God. Although there are numerous verses that speak of the joy we have in Christ now, there are rewards that will be experienced not in this life, but in the next. Let us remind you of what the Bible says about those who serve God with their whole heart.

> . . . as servants of God we commend ourselves in every way; in great endurance; in troubles, hardships and distress; in beatings, imprisonments and riots; in hard work, sleepless nights and hunger; in purity, understanding, patience and kindness; in the Holy Spirit and in sincere love; in truthful speech and in the power of God; with weapons of righteousness in the right hand and in the left; through glory and dishonor, bad report and good report; genuine, yet regarded as imposters; known, yet regarded as unknown; dying, and yet we live on; beaten, and yet not killed; sorrowful, yet always rejoicing; poor, yet making many rich; having nothing, and yet possessing everything (2 Cor 6:4-10).

There's nothing in the passage that gives us either promise or hope that serving God will bring us a sense of personal earthly reward. Clearly, the only reason one is to serve the Lord is simply out of obedience to Him.

The only reason one is to serve the Lord is out of obedience.

Probably the number one reason that ministry professionals leave the ministry is a feeling of "burnout." This occurs primarily when they feel unfulfilled in their professions. When we realize that we serve in the ministry out of our relationship with God, not because it gives us something, the risk of burnout decreases significantly.

Marking Where You Are

1. How does your "call to the ministry" resemble John's?

   _____

   _____

2. Do you believe a "call to the ministry" is the highest calling? If not, why do you think some believe that? If you believe it is, how do you feel about that notion being challenged?

   _____

   _____

3. In writing, describe yourself as you would introduce yourself to someone without telling what you do for a living. When you read it back to yourself, does it sound complete, or is something missing?

   _____

   _____

4. Are there ways that your career in the ministry hinders your relationship with God? If so, what are they?

   _____

   _____

5. If you lost your job today and you needed to change your career, how would that impact your identity?

   _____

   _____

So much of the content of this chapter is devoted to what "call" is not. Let us summarize by clarifying what "call" is. John 15:5 states, "I am the vine; you are the branches. If a man remains in me and I in him, he will bear much fruit; apart from me you can do nothing. . . . This is to my Father's glory, that you bear much fruit, showing yourselves to be my disciples." When God calls us, it is to relationship with Him. It is through abiding in Him—living life step by step with Him—that empowers us to bear fruit in all areas of our lives for the furtherance of the kingdom.

Those who enter the ministry often have a distorted perception of "call" in general, and more specifically of his or her personal "call." Therefore, *the second mark of a healthy ministry professional is that he or she has examined his or "call" and has an understanding of the biblical perspective of "call."*

Chapter Two References

[1] Neil Knierim and Yvonne Burrage, *God's Call: The Cornerstone of Effective Ministry* (Nashville: Convention Press, 2003).

[2] Ibid., 14.

[3] Ray Boltz, "Thank You," *Concert for a Lifetime* (Word Music, 1995).

Boundaries

I don't know the key to success, but I know the key to failure is to try to please everyone.
Bill Cosby

"Let your 'Yes' be 'Yes' and your 'No', 'No'" *(Matt 5:37)*.

Clarifying Relationships with Others

Once upon a time, there was a little sparrow who hated to fly south for the winter. He so intensely dreaded the thought of leaving his home that he decided to delay his departure as long as he could. After bidding a fond farewell to his entire flock of sparrow friends as they flew away, he settled into his comfortable nest for another month.

Finally, the day came when he could no longer endure the bitterness of the coming winter. As the little sparrow took flight towards his southern destination it began to rain. Eventually the rain began to freeze, and as ice formed on his wings he could no longer continue his trip. Almost dead from the cold, he plummeted to earth, landing in a barnyard.

As he breathed what he believed was his last breath, he lamented that he had not heeded the warnings of his friends as they implored him to head south before winter encroached. As he bemoaned his unfortunate lot, a passing cow stopped just above him, lifted its tail, and covered the dying bird in manure.

At first, the little bird could think of nothing except that he was to die in the most humiliating manner ever. However, as the warm manure began to sink into his feathers, it warmed him and life began to return to his body. Feeling hopeful again, he began to sing. His chirping caught the attention of a cat, which quickly came to his aid and began to uncover him. Just as the sparrow began to rejoice in his second chance at living, the cat quickly ate him, swallowing him whole. (Author unknown)

What relevance could this crude and bizarre story about a sparrow have to the topic of being a healthy pastor or, more specifically, to the topic of setting boundaries? There may be several morals to this story; we use it to illustrate only two points.

1. Not everyone who dumps on you is trying to hurt you.
2. Not everyone who takes the load off of you is benefiting you.

It is our opinion that these two points must be engraved under the eyelids of all pastors, or anyone in a helping profession. Stated again: Being helped—really helped—does not always feel good, and "happiness" may not be the feeling that accompanies it. In fact (point 2) a person is not necessarily helped by someone who makes life easier and has fewer expectations.

Much has been written on the subject of boundaries. Drs. Henry Cloud and John Townsend have authored several books on this subject. It is our opinion that their first book *Boundaries* should be required reading for all seminary students. Though we will make reference to their book here, do yourself a favor and read it in its entirety. Ministry professionals often function under the faulty belief that being Christlike means that our first priority is helping people to be happy. We must remember that God does not promise happiness in this life. He does promise joy, but joy usually comes from choosing character over happiness.

Joy usually comes from choosing character over happiness.

We sometimes function under the myth that if we "speak the truth in love" and it stings a little, then we're not doing our job correctly. Helping—serving, ministering to—people is not an easy task. If done properly, it's probably not always an enjoyable task. Without proper boundaries we may lose our vision, purpose, and identity in Christ and soon feel that all our time is spent pleasing those we serve.

Boundaries serve two purposes. The first purpose is to keep things in, and the second is to keep things out. Envision a fence around your home. It allows children to play outside, reducing the risk of their running into the road. They can play freely without worry of where the line between safety and danger lies. By the same token, the fence keeps away other things, such as a roaming dog, that would present danger to the children as they play. Most fenced yards include a gate, which can be opened by an adult to let safe things in or out.

> **Boundaries serve to keep things in and to keep things out.**

So it is with the boundaries we set around ourselves. We can choose whom or what to let in when we know that it is safe. Simply put, boundaries define where we stop, and others begin.

Spread Too Thin

Not long ago I (John) decided that I was too cheap to pay a professional, so I embarked on one of my least favorite house projects: painting. We decided that we would cover the stark white wall in our kitchen and dining room with a rich maroon paint. It felt rewarding to make such a drastic change and I believed that covering a light color with a dark one would be an easy job.

When the painting was completed, I stood back and admired my handiwork and was pleased. However, before I put away my brushes and rollers, I decided to inspect it up close. I saw many places where the paint had gone on too thin. As it dried, it began to look horrible. Although the walls were covered with paint to some degree, there was no way anyone would consider it acceptable. It took a fair measure of work—several additional coats—to fully cover the thinly painted areas.

Being spread too thin can become a way of life for those in professional ministry. Even though it is considered a hazard of the profession, it is sometimes viewed as a measure of doing a good job. However, just like the paint on my dining room walls, a ministry leader spread too thin may cover everything and still not be doing a very good job.

My first twenty years in ministry were spent in youth ministry. Young people typically ask their youth minister to do things: come to my concert, watch my football game, take me to hear this great band, and such. It was easy for me to get caught up in all that was asked of me. It was difficult to say no.

In my current role as church administrator, I face a similar expectation. On a recent Wednesday night I had a 7:00 P.M. Child Development Center meeting, as well as a 7:00 P.M. Building Committee meeting, and a 7:00 P.M. Finance Committee meeting. On the way to these meetings, I was ushered aside by a member of the Personnel Committee who wanted to ask me some questions. Being late to three meetings is quite an accomplishment. Spread too thin? I didn't want to focus on that. Our own belief that we must be "super human," coupled with the denial of our limitations, is a fallacy that WE perpetuate. Although I may have little control over the timing of these three meetings on the same night, most of my scheduling is within my control. When I am spread too thin, it is my fault.

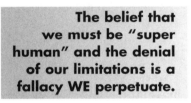

The belief that we must be "super human" and the denial of our limitations is a fallacy WE perpetuate.

It sounds simple enough, but I found setting boundaries difficult at first. Before I took steps to define my boundaries, I had to admit to myself why I was willing to be spread so thin. The first reason was that meeting the needs of others fed my ego as a pastor. Not meeting the needs of others felt as if I was failing. I feared that not meeting everyone's needs would lead to the unemployment line. As I've matured in this area, I have realized that what cripples me in my ministry is not when I get caught in the tug of war of needy people in my church, rather it is when I use my ministry to meet many of my own unhealthy self-esteem needs. When I gave to people, it was often more about meeting my need to feel good about myself than it was about helping others.

The Truth about Happiness

When I (Dan) talk with anyone who wants to become a counselor, whether it is a teenager entering college or an adult starting a graduate program, I invariably hear that the motivation to help others is to lead them to "happiness" or to "feel better." As I age in this profession, I am troubled by this sentiment. Helping people, whether as a counselor or a pastor, is not leading them to feel better or to be happy. Rather, it is to bring those we help to an understanding of what he or she is doing that robs him or her of true joy. This process usually involves facing the ugliness of the unhealthy manner in which he or she lives.

Healing can involve pain. A broken bone has to be set. An infected wound needs to be cleaned. Those seeking to work in helping professions (and the ministry) often find too many rewards in helping people be happy, regardless of the cost. I've had many clients who, over the years, seek my services hoping I'll give permission and bless their desire to leave their marriage because they have found "someone who really makes me happy." In more than one instance I have not seen the person again after I suggest the partner work very hard to honor his or her marriage commitment and face the grueling work necessary to stay married. I am typically challenged by the person with "Surely God would want me to be happy."

Boundaries That Keep Things In

Many people who are drawn to helping professions believe that serving in the ministry will provide a pat on the back. How does this notion become an expectation? Although most would say that the ministry is a career requiring one to sacrifice emotional as well as other tangible rewards, we seem to thrive on the gratitude we get from meeting the perceived spiritual needs of those we serve. Not only do we thrive on the gratitude, but we also come to expect it. When we don't get that gratitude,

> **What reasons have drawn you to the ministry?**

we feel defeated and unappreciated. This can even lead to thinking we are failures. Typically, the cycle is: if I make you happy, then your happiness will make me happy.

First Corinthians 9:22 says, "To the weak I became weak, to win the weak. I have become all things to all men so that by all possible means I might save some." When Paul wrote those words, he evangelized. He met people where they were so that he might be able to reach *some* of them. His philosophy: adjust the approach when evangelizing different groups of people.

Too often we interpret this passage to mean that a ministry professional should be able to meet all the needs of those in his or her ministry. We believe, and allow our congregation to expect, that we are available for every emotional, spiritual, and physical need that they have. We expect and are expected to give personal attention to everyone in the church. It is not reasonable for one person to be able to meet the needs of everyone. To take it a step further, it is not reasonable for one person to connect with all people.

Unhealthy ministries are marked by the belief that if we can meet **all** the needs of those in our congregation then we have succeeded. We condition ourselves to feel good about what we do when those we serve tell us that we have succeeded (e.g., more expectations met = greater success). If they are unhappy with us, then we believe that surely we have failed.

Conflict in the church and in other ministries is inevitable. In normal situations it cannot be avoided. People are fallible so mistakes are made, feelings get hurt, and trust is damaged. Many pastors spend their energy on the trouble spots in the church, but healthy ministry requires us to lead those who can be led. We can only impact those who will allow themselves to be impacted. Often this feels like a double-bind. We should not be afraid of the consequences of actively trying to lead our flock. We need to accept the paradox of being asked to lead while in many cases not being able to do so.

> **Healthy ministry requires us to lead those who can be led.**

Double-Binds

I (John) have served in my current church for thirteen years. It is safe to say that, through these thirteen years, the amount of conflict has quantitatively increased each year. Let's call these unresolved conflicts "baggage." I believe that the longer the tenure at a church, the more baggage the minister will carry. I don't mean this to sound negative and certainly don't believe the remedy is to shorten tenure in order to decrease conflict. Rather, in my thirteen years I have had more people to help carry that baggage and, more importantly, have had people that are willing to accept that I'm not always the cause of conflict but rather the lightning rod. With these people I have also seen faith and trust grow. I respect and am respected, and I have connected with more people. I have found that it is healthier to assign greater power to this second group.

Here are three situations that exemplify common attitudes in congregations that create double-binds for the pastor:

Be all things to all people, but don't get too close.

It was brought to my attention that one of the students in my ministry was abusing alcohol. After praying about whether or not I should intercede, I felt that, for the sake of the young person, I must investigate. I set an appointment with him and confronted him with what I had heard about his drinking. Once he denied its validity, we moved on to a deeper issue. This young man had talked for years about his commitment to God and what he believed was his calling to missions. I pointed out that in spite of his proclaimed passion for missions, he never once joined the youth group on a mission project or trip. Apparently, I hit the nail on the head. In my presence, this young man seethed. His spiritual walk was in bad shape, and he knew that I knew it. He became very emotional, and somewhat taken aback by my perceptiveness in the moment. We concluded our time together with my promise to encourage and cultivate some spiritual healing and accountability.

Later that evening I received a phone call from his father. Irate, he blasted me for accusing his son of being an alcoholic. I was flabbergasted! Of the ninety minutes that I spent with his son that day, we discussed the drinking issue for only ten minutes. I found it amazing that the spiritual aspect of our discussion never made it to the parents' ears. These parents always expected a high level of spirituality from their children. Discussion of God and serving others for Him was commonplace in their home. Perhaps this young person knew that it was safer to tell his parents that I'd accused him of drinking than that I'd confronted him on his lack of spiritual fruit. Simply put, I got too close. People will often let a minister come only so far. Once it is perceived that that invisible line is crossed, watch out. It's as if I was told, "Help me, but not with the real issue."

People will often let a minister come only so far.

Dig into the knee-deep manure of my life, but don't be affected by the smell.

A former client of Dan's that we'll call Chad shared the nightmare all youth pastors dread: the child of someone with whom he'd been close was in trouble. Actually, the teen cried for help and the youth minister chose to respond. This young man had a history of problems, so his father, a good friend of Chad's, encouraged him to be active in his son's spiritual development. Both parents implored Chad to hold their son accountable and to encourage him to share his struggles. Their expectations were clear: they wanted Chad to have a significant impact on their son.

After this young man acted inappropriately on several occasions, Chad asked for a face-to-face meeting with his parents, hoping to get to the bottom of his attitude, demeanor, vulgarity, and downright rude behavior. His concern was met with a pleasant response, but, to his surprise, the family just wanted to ignore the problems. Out of fear that their son was going to smudge their impeccable image, they chose to ignore the seriousness of his needs and instead blamed others in the youth group for mistreating him. The boy's father told Chad, "It's not that bad." So Chad backed off. The behaviors of this troubled adolescent continued, and over time became more severe. Drugs, sex, school suspensions, suicide attempts, and institutionalizations resulted as Chad watched from the sidelines. He had been cautioned by his senior minister not to get involved because the arrogant and image-conscious parents chose not to "smell" what was really going on.

Give me only what I ask for, and only when I want it, but do not give me what I need.

A number of years ago, the senior minister of a large church came to me (Dan) for help with his anger that resulted from a failed attempt to help a prominent family in his congregation. The teenage son had abused drugs and alcohol, got in trouble with the law, dropped out of college, and refused to do anything but sleep all day in his parents' home and party all night using money given to him by his parents.

These parents came to the minister seeking his help. When it became very apparent that their son was not interested in changing his ways, the minister suggested that the parents employ a form of "tough love" which gave the son two months to begin counseling and to find a job and a place to live. The parents agreed and said they would give their son enough money to secure an apartment and pay two months' rent.

In the two months leading to the date their son was to move, these parents asked for enormous amounts of the minister's time, vacillating between venting their anger about their troubled son's actions and struggling with what needed to be done. When the time came for their son to move, they recanted their decision. Instead, they blamed the minister for being too harsh in his expectations, and maligned him to others in the congregation as an uncaring, brutal minister. In order to soothe their own anxieties, they continued to fund their son's partying habit and enabled him to live in their home.

This minister was not only exhausted by this family, but also felt used which led to his own sense of anger and resentment. It was as if he were expected to help, but only to the degree that the hurting person allowed. He realized that the expectation of this family was that he was expected to respond to the crisis, but they didn't really want help to get to the root of the problem and thus eliminate it. He felt as if he was only putting a bandage on an open, infected wound that really needed surgery.

Left unchecked, these dualities will lead us to exhaustion, if not total burnout. We know full well that "the squeaky wheel gets

Believing that we can be all things to all people usually compromises our ministry.

the grease," but by responding only to those who demand our attention, others in great need are neglected. Believing that we can be all things to all people usually compromises our ministry. As a professional minister, I have gifts, education, and expertise. I spend a lot of my time focusing on the spiritual development of those I serve. Often I have found that those in my care want to dictate what I am to do in order to provide a ministry that they want. Too much challenge or too many efforts to move them toward spiritual introspection can result in the complaint, "you're not giving us what we want."

Boundaries That Keep Things Out

Do not make friends with a hot-tempered man;
do not associate with one easily angered. *Proverbs 22:24*

Pastors often agree that this boundary thing sounds great, but doubt that it's applicable for anyone in the ministry. Many ministers believe that they are "owned" by the congregation and should be at any and all member's beck and call.

For example, a pastor was asked to perform the wedding of two members of his church, who were also his friends from college. In the months leading to the wedding, the bride-to-be suffered severe emotional problems, and it was common knowledge among her friends that she not only had a serious drug problem, but also that she was not really ready to get married. Unfortunately, she didn't know how to slow down the process. In premarital counseling with this couple, the mental status of the young woman, as well as the obvious relational conflict, became apparent to the pastor, who decided out of love for this couple that he could not perform the ceremony at that time. He suggested they postpone the wedding so they could address these serious issues. The couple was furious with him.

The wedding took place as planned, but another pastor performed the ceremony. The couple was so upset that their pastor did not set aside his concerns and marry them anyway, they were unwilling to heed the caution of the one person they said they respected.

Remember the story of the sparrow? The couple felt "dumped upon" because their wishes weren't granted. The loving concern expressed by the first pastor may have caused some problems (after all, the reception was planned and the invitations were printed), yet it may have improved the chances of the marriage surviving.

Cloud and Townsend[1] list eight common boundary myths. Any of these myths can be used as attempts to negate the validity of setting boundaries by those who do not want to either set boundaries, or have them set by others.

1. *Setting boundaries means I'm selfish.* The myth here is that, by setting boundaries, we are in fact more concerned about ourselves than we are about giving to others. In reality, a person with good boundaries has a greater chance of being of assistance to others. Even Jesus set a boundary when he left the masses to be alone with His Father (Matt 14:22-23).

2. *Boundaries are a sign of disobedience.* We are often told that if we don't go along with what the church or its leadership wants, then we're being disobedient or rebellious. However, the opposite is more true. When we say "yes" to something when we really want to say "no," we're not being honest. Those without boundaries often are compliant on the outside, but harbor resentment on the inside.

3. *If I begin setting boundaries, others will hurt me.* Although listed as a myth, there is some truth here. When a boundary is set, some may become angry and resent the boundary. This may lead to people withdrawing from and/or neglecting the person setting the boundary. Cloud and Townsend suggest setting boundaries first in those relationships that are safe and healthy. Having such boundaries in relationships will help strengthen your resolve when

others balk at the boundaries you set and punish you for setting them.

4. *If I set boundaries, I will hurt others.* Boundaries are a defensive tool, not an offensive weapon. Some will accuse you of hurting them by setting boundaries, but do not allow them to step over the boundaries. In reality, it is more loving to be clear about what others can expect from us. It is much easier to show love when we feel heard and respected.

5. *Boundaries mean that I'm angry.* In actuality, it is the opposite that is true. Those who do not set boundaries then feel controlled by others and typically become very angry.

6. *I am injured when others set boundaries.* We can be devastated when we want something from someone and do not receive it. If this is something that has occurred in your life, especially in childhood, then you are prone to believe that another's boundary is equal to neglect. Feeling rejected by another's healthy boundary is an indication of something within you that needs attention. Being told "no" does not need to be perceived or experienced as a rejection.

7. *Boundaries cause feelings of guilt.* When setting a boundary, you may be met with, "After all I've done for you, and you're doing this to me?" Others use guilt to invalidate the boundary setting. It is not the boundary that causes feelings of guilt, but rather the person who resists the boundary.

8. *Boundaries are permanent, and I'm afraid of burning my bridges.* You must remember that you own your "no." If you set a boundary in response to another's unhealthy demands, you are free to remove or alter the "no" when the other responds in a healthier manner.

Protecting Yourself from Toxic People

A few years ago I (John) was embattled by parents of several teens in my youth group. I was trying to move these kids to a deeper level of commitment in their spiritual walk, and their parents resisted based on their belief that church should not expect the same level of commitment that school, sports, band, or dance does. In my frustration I went to another pastor, hoping for some support, encouragement, and backing to do the right thing. His only counsel was to not upset these parents. He also reminded me that "Iron sharpens iron" (Prov 27:17). I'm not exactly sure how he intended to encourage me with that Scripture, but I wanted to respond with, "Yeah, iron sharpens iron, but you can get tetanus from a rusty nail."

I'm sure that all of us have numerous experiences with difficult people. Our profession leads these folks to us. A common belief in a congregation of any size is that each church member is the minister's boss or supervisor. The unspoken attitude is, "How dare you say no to *me*?" We are expected to cater to each individual's whim, be on call for each individual crisis, and minister to each member in the way he or she wants to be ministered to. We have been led to believe that any dissatisfaction expressed by parishioners must be taken as constructive criticism, and we must change to please them. This is a deadly trap, unhealthy not only for the pastor but also for the parishioner.

A healthy attitude about church membership is that of ownership. In essence, if I join a church, then I'm going to have a certain degree of ownership that makes me responsible for the work of the church. However, when ownership leads to an attitude of entitlement, unhealthiness ensues. Examples of entitlement include a belief that as a member, *I* can use the facilities anyway *I* want. If *I* believe the King James Version of the Bible is the *only* Bible, then the pastor better not deviate from that version. If the sanctuary is too cold for *me*, then someone should do something about it. If *I* want something from the pastor, then *I* should get it—day or night.

For the purpose of this book, a toxic person is defined as one who has a strong negative or poisonous impact on another. The person who would fit this description is bent towards always finding the negative in a situation or person. This person tends to suck the life out of those with whom he or she comes in contact. The toxic one is usually self-centered, usually has an air of hostility and

> **Unfortunately, the church is full of toxic people.**

neediness, and requires others to agree with him or her. Typically the toxic person functions out of legalism and dogma, rather than embracing the concept of grace. Unfortunately, the church is full of toxic people, and by default the pastor is usually left to deal with them.

As I think about the situations in which I have found myself with toxic people, I must admit that a major problem for me is worrying about who will "cover my back" if, in doing the right thing, I upset people. I am not a vindictive person. It is my desire for peace and harmony among those that I serve. That does not mean that others always perceive me that way. Toxic people believe that they can question the motives of their minister, and that, in so doing, the minister must mold himself to their desires. If the minister doesn't concede, then he is perceived as inflexible, unapproachable, or uncaring.

As previously discussed, most pastors and other church leaders often start out as people pleasers. It is very difficult for people to upset the apple cart when they get their identities and validation from making people happy. But how ridiculous is it to believe that one person can keep a 1200 member congregation happy? In most, if not all, situations where ministry leaders feel "owned" by their congregations, it is the leader who allows, enables, and even encourages this through his or her lack of boundaries.

Dual Relationships

(Dan:) Those of us in the counseling profession have a boundary prescribed for us in our code of ethics. We are cautioned against having "dual relationships" with those we help in a professional setting. The American Association of Christian Counselors Code of Ethics says this about dual relationships:

> Dual relationships involve the breakdown of proper professional or ministerial boundaries. A dual relationship is where two or more roles are mixed in a manner that can harm the counseling relationship. Examples include counseling plus personal, fra-

ternal, business, financial, or sexual and romantic relations...The Rule of Dual Relationships: While in therapy, or when counseling relations are imminent, or for an appropriate time after termination of counseling, Christian counselors do not engage in dual relations with counselees. Some dual relationships are always avoided—sexual or romantic relations and counseling close friends or family member, employees, or supervisees. Other dual relationships should be presumed troublesome and avoided whenever possible.

The Rule of Dual Relationships is primarily designed to protect the client. However, it also protects the counselor by making it very clear to the client what will constitute the relationship with the counselor. While it is impractical to believe that church leaders can have the same rigid boundaries that separate their personal and professional relationships with parishioners, there is some wisdom in limiting emotional intimacy.

There is some wisdom in limiting emotional intimacy.

Pastors are wise if they adopt a personal policy regarding their relationships with church members. At the very least, it is healthy for clergy to regard their parishioners as "clients" of sorts. Sharing too much personal information, having an open door policy in the minister's home, and allowing church members to meet the minister's needs are dangerous and should be avoided. A pastor should use extreme caution in giving total and complete trust or power to a person under his ministry. At the very least, this limits the amount of hurt that will inevitably be caused if a church member becomes toxic in his or her dealings with the pastor.

Guidelines for Maintaining Boundaries

We can't possibly compose an entire list of the boundaries that are appropriate or necessary for the health of ministry leaders. However, here are a few that address the most common boundary issues that ministry professionals face.

Do not look to those in your care to meet your need for validation.

Most of the time a pastor will have numerous people in his congregation who freely show love and respect to him. A good sermon, an appreciated visit to someone in the hospital, or a kind touch of sympathy after a death evokes praise from the church member involved. It becomes easy to minister to those who are appreciative and willing to express such feelings. As a result, it is easy for the pastor to begin to expect such expression to validate not only his ministry, but also his personhood. While these expressions of gratitude are for the most part genuine, there is danger in counting on these accolades as the only diet for validation.

It is essential that the ministry professional receives his majority of *external* validation from family and close friends, so that if problems arise at church, the source of such validation is not in jeopardy. In order to do this, he must become aware of his needs and emotional cravings, as well as what would tempt him to receive this validation from someone within the church.

Avoid dual relationships when possible.

This boundary is one that requires some flexibility. Socialization (a.k.a. fellowship) is very much a part of being in a church, but one should be cautious in entering into business relationships with church members. Using members for attorneys, doctors, mechanics, tax accountants, therapists, home construction, and the like is certainly not out of the question. However, should any of these roles create conflict or problems it can make church relations very difficult.

Limit emotional intimacy with church members.

Being a pastor or member of a pastor's family can be very lonely. (This is addressed in the next chapter.) Many pastors are willing to share the details of past and present personal life, hoping it will help a parishioner in some way. This can lead to significant problems, and in the end does not help either party.

Pastors, like everyone, need people with whom they can vent, share concerns, and go to when they need nurture and emotional care. It is dangerous at best to invest such depth into the average church member. Deep relationships with church members where the pastor is to receive (more than give) need significant forethought, prayer, and wisdom prior to the risk.

Trust in a church member cannot be given lightly. I (John) remember early in my ministry when I experienced conflict with my senior pastor who was speaking about my performance to the members of the personnel committee. In my congregation there was one youth worker who was aware of the situation and identified himself as my ally and confidante, or so I thought. I later discovered that what I entrusted with him was in turn reported to the pastor. I learned that trusting a church member is risky, because when church conflict ensues, it brings out the worst in people.

It may be that you find your most trusted confidante in your congregation. This is not taboo, but you should be aware of potential hazards. Unfortunately, your closest confidante may not be your best ally when there is church conflict, as others may disqualify that person because he or she is "too close" to you.

Declare what's off-limits for public knowledge.

It's unfortunate that most churches publish every detail of the minister's salary. Privacy in such matters is afforded to other careers, but not to those in the ministry.

There are issues of life that the minister and his family have the ability and responsibility to regulate. Vacations plans, housing choices, where the kids attend school, and who they spend personal time with are all examples of things that do not need approval or foreknowledge from the congregation. Although the ministry professional—as well as the rest of us—needs to live a life consistent with Christlike principles, how a minister spends his personal time or money is not the business of the congregation.

Make your marriage and family's privacy a priority.

It is perfectly acceptable to let the answering machine screen your calls! All too often church members would prefer to call a minister at home to deal with something that is more appropriately dealt with during office hours. In such an instance, an appropriate response would be, "This is a very important issue, and I want to give it my full attention. Please call me tomorrow at my office and I'll be glad to address it then."

Fortunately, most ministers no longer live in parsonages next to the church. When that was tradition, parishioners felt at liberty to show up at any time and invade the pastor's home. This violation of privacy was undoubtedly the source of marital and family conflict. It is an unhealthy mistake to allow your home to be a place where church members can feel entitled to show up regularly unannounced. Since ministers and their families are often "under the microscope" (so to speak), it is essential that home life is off limits to the rest of the church.

A family that is protected by healthy boundaries is one that can actually "rest." Without the scrutiny of being "under the microscope" a minister's family enjoys the same privacy as other families. They can have fights and squabbles among themselves. Adolescent children can struggle with rebellion (that all healthy adolescents go through) without the implied expectation that the minister's kids are to be examples for all the kids in the congregation. Boundaries

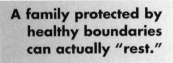

A family protected by healthy boundaries can actually "rest."

also allow the minister and his family to take a break from their roles in the church. This allows for development of other aspects of family life, and enables the minister to be rejuvenated when he steps into his public role.

Honor your vacations and days off.

Church work creates a crazy schedule. Working on Sundays and evening meetings and visitations require church leaders to work varying hours of the day and varying days of the week. For this reason alone, it is imperative that ministry professionals honor their days off and take all the vacation time they are given. This may require another pastor to do a funeral if a death occurs during a family trip. Another church leader may need to visit a parishioner in the hospital if it's the minister's day off. A fairly rigid policy regarding time off actually pays dividends to the church: a rested minister who is better able to fulfill the tasks of his job. A well-rested pastor who takes time off regularly is not only in better shape, but also is less likely to take unexpected time off.

Be clear in what others can expect from you.

It is commonplace for a church member to request a church leader's attention at the busiest times. Before Sunday's worship service, in the church parking lot, or even the grocery store are all places that seem to declare "open season" on the pastor. As a ministry professional you must get in the habit of responding consistently, much like stated previously: "Thank you for bringing that to my attention. I'm preoccupied at the moment and I'm afraid I can't give you enough time. Please, call my office in the morning and we'll schedule a time to get together soon." Although some may be offended at what they perceive as being put off, soon they will come to respect your boundary and demand such attention less frequently.

Church members readily believe that they are the only ones served by the minister. Many become insulted if the minister doesn't visit often enough, attend family members' weddings, or respond to numerous other requests. For this reason it is the minister's responsibility to decline invitations and requests when he needs or wants to. Telling someone that you'll try to be there when you know you probably won't only hinders your integrity. It is the minister's responsibility to educate his church members about his limitations because congregations tend to believe ministers thrive on meeting their needs. A minister who lets his congregants know the limits of his abilities and time not only sets a more appropriate expectation, but also lets those in his care know that it's okay to set limits.

> **A minister who lets his congregants know his limits also permits them to set limits.**

Marking Where You Are

1. What are some of the things that you need your boundaries to keep in, and what needs to be kept out?

   _____

   _____

2. Reread the story of the little sparrow. Do you have people in your life who play the role of the cow and the cat? Which of the two are more trustworthy?

   _____

   _____

3. What are the common issues in your life and church that you believe cannot be addressed or changed?

   _____

   _____

4. Which of the eight common boundary myths as described by Cloud & Townsend are you most inclined to use to keep from setting boundaries? What can you do to change this?

   _____

   _____

5. If you were on a family vacation and someone in your congregation died, would you return early to do the funeral? What factors go into making that decision? Are those factors really healthy?

   _____

   _____

The Third Mark

The sparrow in the story exhibited a common trait of human nature. We want to live life on our own terms. We often choose to ignore the wisdom of God and those He places around us, only to find ourselves in dire straits. We then choose to believe that being helped out of difficult situations should come with little cost or consequence.

As people helpers it is imperative that we don't respond to people with "what they want," but rather "what they need." This is best accomplished when we are in tune with our own needs, and have set appropriate boundaries around ourselves. *The third mark of a healthy ministry professional is that he or she has learned to set and maintain boundaries.*

Chapter Three Reference

[1] Henry Cloud and John Townsend, *Boundaries* (Grand Rapids: Zondervan, 1992).

Friendship

Be courteous to all, but intimate with few, and let those few
be well tried before you give them your confidence.
George Washington

Wounds from a friend can be trusted, but an enemy multiplies kisses *(Prov 27:6)*.

Lonely in the Crowd

Pastors are often lonely, knowing neither the limits nor the benefits of deep relationship with others. Most are surprised at the degree of loneliness they experience. They believe that working in a profession that is focused on people would be the last career that fosters loneliness. Deeper probing reveals that the reason ministers feel so alone is that they don't have friends. Well, maybe they have friends, but they typically do not cultivate deep, meaningful relationships with others. Further exploration into this fact elicits these universal reasons or excuses:

A pastor is not supposed to have friends. If he does, then it causes problems within the church.

Loyalty to one or a few within a congregation leads to jealousy of other members.

A pastor is supposed to be there for everyone, and if he spends time and effort on cultivating a meaningful personal relationship with someone, this limits what he can do for everyone else.

In the previous chapter we discussed the need to set boundaries that keep a healthy distance between the pastor and those he serves. It might seem inconsistent, then, to put such a high priority on a friendship. The deepest friendship that we describe herein is one that may occur only once in a lifetime. It probably can't be duplicated as the pastor moves from church to church. Problems may arise if this type of relationship occurs within the congregation that he serves. Although friendship involves give and take, the minister needs a friendship where he often receives more than he gives.

> **Although friendship involves give and take, the minister needs a friendship where he often receives more than he gives.**

The Difficulty for Ministers

I (John) have always been a people person. Throughout my life I have had a long list of people that I considered my friends. As I've aged, I don't think the number of those that I've counted as friends has decreased. I do know, however, that through my adult years in the ministry I continued to feel increasingly isolated and lonely. As I began to deal with various issues in my life, I came to realize that I believed that, as a pastor, I could not have a deep, meaningful relationship with anyone other than my wife. Although my relationship with her is the most important in my life, and the depth of that relationship is essential to my well being, it can't meet all of my needs. In fact, my neediness can be detrimental to my wife if I'm not careful. I also realize that I believed everyone in my ministry was my friend, so feeling lonely didn't make sense.

Throughout ministry I've known of several instances where someone who was "too close" to the minister caused problems. When I look back on each of those, I realize that it wasn't necessarily the relationship that was unhealthy. Rather, it was the congregation, or a few unhappy church members, who decided that it wasn't what they felt was necessary for the mental health of their pastor.

To keep from too much intimacy in relationships, ministry professionals seem to function by these rules of friendship:

The more the merrier. The justification here is that, if I claim to have a lot of friends, and I'm liked by a lot of people, then that must make me a good person. Conversely, if only a few people like me, then something must be wrong with me. The need to have a large group of people around me ensures that surely someone will be there for me when the others aren't. The fallacy of this rule is that friendship becomes more about outward appearance than about inward investment.

There is safety in numbers. If I have a great number of friends, then I really can't invest myself to any depth with any one of them. If I spread myself too thin, then certainly no one will get to know me, and I won't have to be as vulnerable.

The Challenge for Ministers

As you read this chapter, keep in mind that the purpose herein is to help you understand that there are limits to all relationships. I (Dan) know many ministers who believed that those under his care would remain loyal under any circumstance, only to discover the relationships were very weak when the minister was in need. For the sake of your needs and to ensure that your wounds receive care, I encourage you to invest in deep relationships that are orchestrated by God.

There are limits to all relationships.

Friendship Defined

John and I differ in whom we call "friend." John is quick to refer to anyone with whom he interacts regularly as "my friend." I, on the other hand, reserve that title for deeper relationships. In other words, the title "friend" is open for interpretation.

When we classify all with whom we have relationship as "friends," it is difficult to know what we can expect from them, and what they want from us. Failure to distinguish degrees of friendship can lead to all relationships being the same, therefore robbing us of the deepest, most committed forms of friendship. For this reason, we have broken "friendship" into the following categories: acquaintances, colleagues, close friends, and sworn friends.

> **Failure to distinguish degrees of friendship can rob us of the deepest, most committed forms.**

Acquaintances

This category would include those people with whom we regularly associate, but have little or no commitment to beyond the environment where we associate, for instance, a classmate, a church member we say "hello" to every Sunday, the parents of our children's friends, and the like. We may or may not know their names, even though we may interact with these people daily. However, outside of the environment where the interaction occurs, we have no commitment to these people.

Colleagues

These people are in our lives for a specific purpose. Coworkers with whom we socialize at work would fit into this category, as would someone we play with on a team. Our relationship with these folks is based upon a common interest. The depth of the relationship lies within the context of this common interest.

Close Friends

Included in this category would be those people who have a significant influence upon us. We share many things with them. The relationship goes beyond common interests or common environments. People with whom we remain connected even when we're not in regular contact with them will be in this category. Most family relationships fit in here as well.

Sworn Friends

Using the relationship of David and Jonathan helps define this unique and extraordinary friendship. A sworn friend is one who is committed to God's plan for your life and is willing to invest heavily to bringing this plan to reality.

Sworn Friendships in the Bible

Of all the friendships in the Scriptures, the one shared by David and Jonathan is best known.

Jonathan was the most eligible bachelor in all of Israel. He would someday be king, and every facet of his life was directed at preparing him for his destiny. This came to a screeching halt one day as he stood with his father, Saul, observing the army of Israel as it camped across from the Philistines. David was but a shepherd boy with the courage to attempt a nearly impossible feat. Jonathan watched as David killed the mighty giant Goliath.

Later, Jonathan heard rumors that David was anointed with oil by the prophet Samuel, who proclaimed that God had removed His hand from Saul, and that David was going to be the next king of Israel.

No one could have blamed Jonathan had he been jealous. His entire life had been spent in preparation for his eventual kingship. He was counting on it, and now it was taken from him and given to a lowly shepherd boy. Instead, Jonathan accepted that David was to be king. In an act of submission and recognition of David's position, Jonathan removed his robe, tunic, sword, bow, and belt and gave them to David, and "Jonathan made a covenant with David because he loved him as himself" (1 Sam 18:3). This covenant made by Jonathan did not happen after building a relationship with David. Rather, it occurred instantaneously as Jonathan decided to be a friend (not mentor, advisor, or coworker, but friend) to David.

> **Jonathan willingly gave up his birthright because he believed in God's call of David.**

"There was an immediate bond of love between them. Jonathan swore to be his blood brother, and sealed the pact by giving him his robe, sword, bow, and belt" (1 Sam 18:1, TLB).

The Scripture indicates that Jonathan willingly gave up his birthright because he believed in God's call on David's life. He would have had his father's support in attempting to challenge David, but he instead chose to respond to the truth about David's path.

Jonathan was groomed to believe that the legacy he would leave was to come from being king of Israel. Because he chose to listen to God's plan that David be king, his legacy was that of being a sworn friend instead. Later in the story of these friends, Jonathan offers to David "Whatever you want me to do, I'll do for you" (1 Sam 20:4). Jonathan knew that David was in need of help. He was unwavering in his conviction of God's call on David's life and had no difficulty in promising to do *whatever* he needed of him. David was alone and on the run to save his own life. Jonathan was there for him, recommitting his promise to David. "And Jonathan had David reaffirm his oath out of love for him, because he loved him as he loved himself" (v. 17). Later, when they parted ways, "Jonathan said to David, 'Go in peace, for we have sworn friendship with each other in the name of the LORD, saying, "The LORD is witness between you and me, and between your descendants and my descendants forever"'" (1 Sam 20:42). In essence, "You can go with the assurance that I will remain committed to you long after we pass from this life."

Jonathan eventually died fighting a military battle that amounted to nothing; the greatest accomplishment of his life was recognizing God's purpose for David's life and committing his friendship to David. He kept his covenant with David even until the end.

> **The greatest accomplishment of Jonathan's life was recognizing and committing to God's purpose for David's life.**

The relationship between Jonathan and David is a prime example of a sworn friendship, but it's not the only one. The Bible gives significant credibility to friendships; there are several examples of committed, sworn friendships throughout the Scriptures. Each relationship contains an element of true friendship that can be used to develop a model of a healthy, healing, and deep friendship. Here are a few:

A sworn friend recognizes and encourages the gifts and purpose of his friend and is willing to go out on a limb to help him fulfill his God-ordained purpose.

In Exodus 7 we read about Moses and his relationship with Aaron. It was Moses' God-ordained job to deliver the people of Israel. At a time when Moses was losing strength in this enormous task, Aaron came alongside him and used his own strength to deliver a message to Pharaoh. This came at a cost to Aaron, who did so willingly for the love of Moses.

A sworn friendship is deeper than a friendship based upon mutually shared interests or a relationship through marriage.

Ruth 1–4 tells the story of a relationship between a mother and daughter-in-law. Naomi was widowed and was left with two sons. Her sons both married, and later they died also. After the loss of her family, Naomi left the place she had been living to return to the land of Judah. Naomi instructed her daughters-in-law to return to their homelands and families. Though they both wept at the prospect of leaving Naomi, only one of them returned to her people. The second one, Ruth, pleaded with her beloved mother-in-law and friend, "Don't urge me to leave you or to turn back from you. Where you go I will go, and where you stay I will stay. Your people will be my people and your God my God. Where you die I will die, and there I will be buried. May the LORD deal with me, be it ever so severely, if anything but death separates you and me" (Ruth 1:16-17).

This passage of Scripture is often used in marriage ceremonies, and many naively believe this describes the same covenant made between husband and wife. Not so. Ruth's commitment to Naomi extended beyond what would be expected. Her commitment to Naomi was based purely on love and loyalty. She remained with Naomi, even under very difficult circumstances.

Sworn friendships encourage openness that inspires.

Elisha, who was Elijah's personal attendant and friend, was to eventually assume Elijah's role as leading prophet. As the time drew near that Elijah was to die, Elisha was encouraged to separate from him. Three times Elisha boldly stated, "I will not leave you!" (2 Kings 2). Being with Elijah enabled Elisha to grow. When Elijah asked, "What can I do for you before I am taken from you?" Elisha answered, "Let me inherit a double portion of your spirit." In sworn friendships we not only encourage each other to develop our strengths and gifts, but we emanate those qualities of the other. After Elijah's death, Elisha performed twice as many miracles as did Elijah.

Sworn friends expect the best of each other. They encourage each other to have courage and to stand for what is right regardless of the cost.

At a time when Israel was crumbling, Joshua and Caleb (Numbers 14) were sent along with others as spies to determine if the land of Canaan could be conquered. Upon their return only Joshua and Caleb believed the land could be Israel's, while the others disputed what they believed. Joshua and Caleb continued to encourage one another to hold fast to their convictions and, in the end, were proven right.

A sworn friend, through wisdom and a connection with God, encourages us to be our authentic selves.

Paul readily recognized Timothy's giftedness. When people questioned Timothy's abilities and doubted his maturity, Paul was an advocate for him. Paul was willing to see what God created in Timothy and admonished him, "Don't let anyone look down on you because you are young, but set an example for the believers in speech, in life, in faith and in purity." (1 Tim 4:12) This in turn gave Timothy the encouragement and blessing to live out his purpose.

A sworn friend will stand by you when you have done wrong and will allow you to face the consequences, even if it brings him or her personal loss.

In the book of Philemon we read in Paul's letter of his love and concern for Onesimus. He refers to his friend as "my very heart" (v. 12) and is asking that Onesimus be freed from his role as slave. Paul continues, "So if you con-

Paul is willing to take his role as sworn friend to the extent that he would pay Onesimus's debt.

sider me a partner, welcome him as you would welcome me. If he has done you any wrong or owes you anything, charge it to me" (vv. 17-18). Paul is willing to take his role as sworn friend to the extent that he would pay the debt of Onesimus.

Another example of this is found in Acts. Barnabas remained true to his friendship with John Mark, even though it cost him favor with Paul. "Some time later Paul said to Barnabas, 'Let's go back and visit the brothers in all the towns where we preached the word of the Lord and see how they are doing.' Barnabas wanted to take John, also called Mark, with them, but Paul did not think it wise to take him, because he had deserted them in Pamphylia and had not continued with them in the work. They had such a sharp disagreement that they parted company. Barnabas took Mark and sailed for Cyprus, but Paul chose Silas and left, commended by the brothers to the grace of the Lord" (Acts 15:36-40).

Jesus and His Friendships

Jesus invested in relationships as well. During His ministry years He surrounded Himself with a chosen twelve. Although He shared a significant relationship with His disciples, He was not deeply connected with all of them. What can we learn from Jesus in terms of His friendships? Can we be as bold to say that Jesus probably had a best friend? A sworn friend? John is referred to as the disciple whom Jesus loved (John 19:26). There are at least five other passages in John where reference is made to "the disciple whom Jesus loved" (John 13:23; 19:26; 20:2; 21:7,20). Though it does not mention anyone by name in these verses, we can assume that it is indeed John. Not only does this lend credibility to the notion that we all have those in our lives whom we love more than others; it also legitimizes the fact that this does not need to be kept secret.

> **Not only can we have those in our lives whom we love more than others, but this does not need to be kept secret.**

What does the Bible say about the way Jesus related to His friends?

He had expectations for those who loved Him.

In the last hours of His life, Jesus asked His disciples to pray with Him, and when they failed to do as He asked, He expressed His disappointment with them.

"Then Jesus went with his disciples to a place called Gethsemane, and he said to them, 'Sit here while I go over there and pray.' He took Peter and the two sons of Zebedee along with him, and he began to be sorrowful and troubled. Then he said to them, 'My soul is overwhelmed with sorrow to the point of death. Stay here and keep watch with me.' . . . Then he returned to his disciples and found them sleeping. 'Could you men not keep watch with me for one hour?' he asked Peter. . . . He went away a second time and prayed. . . . When he came back, he again found them sleeping, because their eyes were heavy. So he left them and went away once more and prayed the third time. . . . Then he returned to the disciples and said to them, 'Are you still sleeping and resting?'" (Matt 26:36-45).

When it gave honor to God, Jesus gave special treatment to those He loved the most.

In John 11 we read of the death of Lazarus. Verse 3 reveals the message given to Jesus: ". . . the one you love is sick." Although Jesus knew that He would raise Lazarus from the dead, He was deeply moved at Mary's grief (v. 33) and responded by weeping (v. 35). His visible display of grief caused those around Him to say, "See how he loved him!" He then brought Lazarus to life again.

Listen closely: Jesus raised Lazarus to bring honor to His Father. But by the same token, those who were watching knew that Jesus loved Lazarus, and they knew that Jesus chose to perform a miracle for His friend.

He was willing to show love by caring for the unpleasant parts of His friends.

Look at His act of service when He washed the disciples' feet (John 13). This task was one usually done by a servant for the master or guest. In this instance, Jesus washes the feet of His disciples as an object lesson about serving others. This was not a pleasant task. However, Jesus tended lovingly to the lowly parts of those He loved.

My Friendship with Dan

In my situation, the birth of a sworn friendship came from recognizing that I (John) was in a bad place. I probably didn't spend enough time praying about how to find healing, but I did feel a leading to open up to someone safe. Unknown to me, God had already begun to prepare Dan to be a sworn friend. Slow and deliberate investment into that friendship created an environment in which I was able to look honestly at myself for the first time in my life.

Our friendship parallels that of Jonathan and David in many ways. Dan is very much the Jonathan in our relationship. He quickly and continually sees through to the core of me. He knows my weaknesses and readily points them out to me. He believes in me and acknowledges my gifts and talents and holds me accountable to use them.

In my ministry he has been an extra pair of hands. He continually reminds me that I need to take care of myself if I am to be of any ministerial good to others. He is a thorn in my side on a regular basis, reminding me to stay focused and to keep my personal issues from getting in the way of the work for which God has created me. He expects the best from me and allows me to get angry with him for it. He tends to my wounds and nurtures me when appropriate. My relationship with him and his consistency with me is something on which I've come to depend. It's one of the few things on my "What I know for sure" list.

Because Dan is a member of the church that I now serve, our friendship has caused the typical problems that we described earlier. This has made it necessary to be very clear with boundaries and has even limited Dan's ability to serve in certain capacities within the church. I fully expect our relationship to remain a sworn friendship if or when the time comes that either of us leaves for another church.

My Friendship with John

I (Dan) agree with John when he states that I am very much the "Jonathan" in our friendship. I think the distinct differences in our personalities are essential for the David/Jonathan dynamic to work; we believe that the nature of this relationship reflects that Jonathan served David. By nature, John is a gregarious person: more out in front and thriving in the limelight. I am more comfortable functioning in the shadows. I tend to rely more on my intuition and my other senses as I observe, while John is usually at the center of activity and interaction. However, just as we see in Scripture, John and I have a mutual respect and love for one another.

As I look at Jonathan's role with David, I find three things that are essential to their relationship that hold true to ours:

Jonathan was certain of the special anointing that David had been given.

You will recall that it was Jonathan who was in line for the throne. However, Samuel anointed David who would later become king. There is no reference in Scripture to Jonathan's fighting this. It's as if he also sensed this special direction for David's life. He then fashioned his own life around helping David achieve his status.

You will recall in this book's introduction that the onset of my relationship with John came from my sensing a special anointing from God on his life. Before I knew John well, I was led to pray for him and affirm this unique quality.

Jonathan's loyalty to David surpassed even that of loyalty to family.

In 1 Samuel 19:1-2 we read, "Saul told his son Jonathan and all the attendants to kill David. But Jonathan was very fond of David and warned him, 'My father Saul is looking for a chance to kill you. Be on your guard tomorrow morning; go into hiding and stay there.'" Later in chapter 20:1-2 David asks, "'What have I done? What is my crime? How have I wronged your father, that he is trying to take my life?' 'Never!' Jonathan replied. 'You are not going to die! Look, my father doesn't do anything, great or small, without confiding in me. Why would he hide this from me? It's not so!'" Later, Jonathan devised an elaborate plan to fool his father in order to protect David.

The loyalty displayed here supersedes the old cliché "Blood is thicker than water." If necessary, my relationship with John would also need to model a loyalty that outlives family tension.

Jonathan vowed to do whatever he could for David.

Jonathan swears to David in 1 Samuel 20:4, "Whatever you want me to do, I'll do for you." This was not a lighthearted prom-

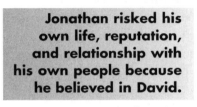
Jonathan risked his own life, reputation, and relationship with his own people because he believed in David.

ise. Jonathan risked his own life, reputation, and relationship with his own people because he believed in David. Jonathan made it his ministry (so to speak) to advance God's plan for his friend.

As Jonathan was to David, I am committed to doing whatever John needs for me to do for him, providing that doing so would be God-honoring.

Marking Where You Are

1. Across the top of a page of paper, list the headings: Acquaintances, Colleagues, Close Friends, and Sworn Friends. List the names of those under each category. Examine the number of names under each. What does this tell you about yourself?

   _____

   _____

2. How have friends been a benefit and a hindrance to your ministry?

   _____

   _____

3. If you have a sworn friendship, are you a David or a Jonathan? How do you feel about that?

   _____

   _____

4. Do you have relationships that are too risky? In other words, have you trusted those who are not really trustworthy? If so, what is it about you that enables that to happen?

   _____

   _____

5. Using Jesus' response to his friends, write a description of the type of friend you want to be.

   _____

   _____

The Fourth Mark

The difficulty in writing this chapter is that it might be taken as a suggestion that one should set out to find a sworn friend.

There is no formula to do so, and, in fact, the very thought of orchestrating such a relationship almost cheapens the friendship.

We believe it to be important for you to have a clear understanding of your relationships. Often, as in John's case, it's easy to believe that someone who is an *acquaintance* is a *close friend*. We have heard all too often instances in which someone (not only a minister) has chosen to invest and disclose in a relationship that didn't warrant such a measure of trust. When we are unclear of the depth of a specific relationship, it is easy to either expect or risk too much, which can be damaging for both parties.

At the same time, to be oblivious to a relationship that has the makings of a sworn friendship is to lose out on a unique blessing. Such friendships are rare, and we don't believe we're promised relationships of this nature. If we're given one, it may be a once-in-a-lifetime relationship. We believe, and have experienced, that there is a wealth of scriptural evidence that confirms healthy, committed friendships help us in our ministry, enhance our lives, and are validated by God.

Healthy, committed friendships are validated by God.

The fourth mark of a healthy ministry professional is that he or she understands the limits of most relationships and embraces and values deep friendships.

A Life and Ministry of Integrity

Try not to become a man of success but rather try to become a man of value.
Albert Einstein

There was a man who had two sons. He went to the first and said, "Son, go and work today in the vineyard." "I will not," he answered, but later he changed his mind and went. Then the father went to the other son and said the same thing. He answered, "I will, sir," but he did not go.
Which of the two did what his father wanted? *(Matt 21:28-31)*.

Integrity: The Foundation and Fruit of Wholeness

It is our contention that addressing the four elements outlined in this book will help lead ministers to wholeness. Being "whole" has benefits for each of us, not only as individuals, but also in the roles played in the ministry. What often threatens our wholeness is allowing our integrity to be compromised. Imagine a boat running into a piling that supports a bridge. There may be no visible damage to the bridge itself, yet the integrity—or wholeness—of the bridge is compromised.

A pastor who is whole will naturally base both his life and ministry on integrity. Integrity is both the benefit and the expectation of one who has pursued wholeness.

The root of the word *integrity* is *integer*. Webster defines *integer* as a complete entity, and gives a threefold definition of *integrity*.

1. An unimpaired condition
2. Firm adherence to a code, especially of moral or artistic values
3. The quality or state of being complete or undivided, honest.

In order for the ministry professional to maintain wholeness, he or she must not compromise his or her integrity. Using the threefold definition given by Webster, a person of integrity must have an unimpaired condition (the premise of this book), must adhere to a code of values, and must live in a state of honesty.

"Terminal Uniqueness": The Most Common Threat to Integrity

Before we look at the three parts of integrity, I (Dan) want to consider a condition that roadblocks our understanding and practice of integrity. In my counseling practice I help people who find themselves in varying dilemmas in which they feel stuck, or unable to change. In working through the process of addressing their sufferings and moving towards change, I often hear something like, "I see what you're saying, Dan, and I guess I believe that in someone else's situation that would make sense, but *my situation is so different that I don't believe that applies to me*."

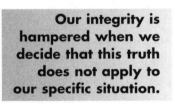

Our integrity is hampered when we decide that this truth does not apply to our specific situation.

Another common response, especially from someone who has suffered a legitimate trauma or violation is, "*You just don't know how bad it is for me.*" Although it's not a clinical diagnosis, at that moment I (tongue in cheek) let my client know that he or she is experiencing an untreatable condition called "Terminal Uniqueness." Our integrity is hampered when we decide that what is true in almost all situations does not apply to our specific situation. Why is integrity affected by this? At its essence, integrity requires one to make choices that can lead to hard work, conflict with others, and maybe even the loss of relationship before the benefits are realized.

I find the affliction of terminal uniqueness to be universally true for ministers who find themselves on the edge of burnout. This evidences itself especially when addressing the second mark regarding "call." After examining the biblical description of call with a minister and even upon his declaration that he believes God calls us to relationship, I regularly hear, "*Yes, I see that, but my situation is different. I believe that I am called to this specific job. God has a task for me to do, and these people in my congregation are standing in my way!*"

Another instance where this is particularly evident is when attempting to help a minister or church leader understand and set boundaries. Again, I rarely (if ever) have someone tell me that he or she believes that setting boundaries is a bad or unbiblical idea. Instead, the common responses I receive are:

✦ *"You don't understand; my congregation is very small, I'm the only minister on staff, so they need me."*

✦ *"I wish I could set boundaries, but in my church the minister always visits everyone in the hospital and everyone who is shut in at home every week. It's tradition."*

✦ *"I have such a burden for lost souls that I could never miss an opportunity to minister to someone."*

✦ *"There are enough problems in my church already; I can only imagine the trouble it will cause for me if I try to set boundaries."*

✦ *"The members of my church are all my bosses, so I can't set boundaries with them."*

At that moment, as counselor, I make it clear to the client that if he believes that to be true, then he will not be able to move forward. Ministry leaders must come to the understanding that terminal uniqueness is an invalid excuse. You cannot have integrity, or wholeness, if you believe that your situation is so unique that God is incapable of changing it through you.

> **You cannot have integrity if you think God cannot change your unique situation.**

Those leaders who have taken the time to work, really work, through their situations are the ones that find wholeness in their lives and a restoration of their ministries. So that is why I ask my clients to deal with the painful issue of terminal uniqueness. They cannot move forward until they come to grips with their own situations and God's desire for how to handle those situations. Integrity can be maintained if we make those difficult decisions. We can live a life that honestly reflects Christ when we refuse to buy into the lie that we are somehow beyond God's help.

The Four Marks and Integrity

Once a ministry professional has worked through each of the four marks we describe in this book and functions with integrity in both personal life and ministry, what does that person look like? In this chapter we'd like to flesh this out.

An Unimpaired Condition:
Physically, Emotionally, and Spiritually

Living at One's Best

Since perfection is not attainable on earth, "living at one's best" most briefly, easily, and accurately describes an unimpaired condition for man. Living in an unimpaired condition, even by this definition, is an ongoing process that, once achieved, requires constant work in order to maintain the desired level of health.

It is unnecessary for us to go into detail regarding the need to take care of ourselves physically. Common sense dictates that eating well, exercising, and getting enough sleep are essential for good physical health. There are resources that address these issues so we don't feel a need to elaborate those points here. We believe it "enough said" to say that if you aren't caring for your body (especially as you age) eventually health problems will invade your life and ministry.

Unfortunately, we don't want to take the same cavalier attitude with emotional and spiritual health. Just as it's easy (though surprising) for a doctor to neglect her physical health or a counselor to ignore his mental or emotional condition, it is easy for a minister to neglect his own spiritual well being. It is not enough spiritual nutrition to prepare a sermon, research and deliver a Bible study, or give spiritual counsel to a parishioner. Most ministers we know struggle with a consistent quiet time, experience overload when they constantly listen to sermons on Christian radio, and feel that interacting with God is a function of their jobs to the point that they spend little to no time developing their personal relationship with God (which, of course, is what they've been called to).

> **You must find a way to connect with God outside of your ministerial duties.**

In order to live at his or her best, the ministry professional must find a way to connect with God outside of his or her ministerial duties. Whether it be in personal retreat or conference, an occasional Sunday off in order to sneak away to another church's (or denomination's) worship service, or seeking time with someone who can act as a mentor, it is essential that the healthy minister ensure his integrity by establishing a deliberate plan for spiritual care. We cannot overemphasize the importance of church leadership, as a whole, nurturing and protecting the minister's health as well. Groups such as the church elders should help the minister by encouraging him to set boundaries, allowing him time to be personally refreshed, and deflecting church criticism by showing the congregation that the church's leaders are a united front.

Emotional (or mental) health is equally as important. For anyone—not just a minister—in a helping profession it is easy to neglect his or her emotional health. Even at our healthiest, old issues from our families of origin and scars from old wounds can surface and knock the wind out of us. If the minister is not constantly aware of these times, then a slow and gradual slide to emotional distress is inevitable. It is imperative that a plan for self-care be in place so that, when a current situation triggers a past issue, the healthy minister knows to whom and where to go for help.

Not Controlled by External Forces

(Dan:) Because of our sins and their consequences we are destined to a life of uphill battles. One of the more difficult battles that we face is when external forces entice our personal, internal desires. Most of our desires (sex, eating, or pleasure of any kind) are not in-and-of themselves wrong. However, outside of the context in which God designed them to be fulfilled these desires can result in sinful behaviors with devastating results. When we allow external forces to lure our internal desires into a sinful or otherwise unhealthy arena, our condition becomes impaired.

We struggle writing this, because so much of what we say is common sense and no one will dispute that even good people are tempted into bad, sinful situations. However, our bent towards terminal uniqueness leads us to believe that it may happen to "someone else" but not to me. Rather than elaborate on the list of vices, unhealthy types of people to avoid, or unhealthy desires, we implore you, the reader, to believe it could happen to you.

> **We are led to think that it may happen to "someone else" but not to us.**

My experience counseling couples who seek my services after one partner has had an affair has taught me that most people who have crossed the line into marital infidelity did not set out to do so. Although there are those situations where this is not the case, for the most part it was a small deviation into dangerous territory that resulted in the affair.

In November 2006 Ted Haggard resigned as leader of the megachurch he started in his basement more than 20 years ago. He resigned because an investigative board formed within his church found him guilty of "sexually immoral conduct" and purchasing illegal drugs.

We do not know much about this man except what has been in the media. We choose to believe that the secret life in which he found himself was one at the bottom of a slippery slope. It's very likely that what started out as a temptation that he thought he could handle ended up being the demise of his ministry and may have left irreparable scars on this family.

External forces are Satan's tools that tempt us to allow our individual bent to sin to become an action, not just a thought. To believe for one second that it could not happen to us is to invite Satan to prove us wrong. It is necessary for anyone who wants to live a life of integrity to take an inventory and remain aware of those areas of danger and then steer clear of them. Also, this is where the support of the church leadership and a sworn friend are so vital to a healthy ministry leader. The elders in a church can help create an environment where the minister can function at a healthy level—for example, protecting the schedule of the minister so that he does not feel an undue amount of stress to perform, which could leave him more vulnerable to the evil one's attacks. A sworn friend can provide accountability and encouragement—asking those hard questions that must be asked and demonstrating grace and forgiveness when errors are made. Surround yourself with people who will help you live the life that God has called you to live, not the cheap imitation of life that Satan tries to sell us.

Surround yourself with people who will help you live authentic rather than imitation life.

Living in the Likeness of Christ

Many years ago I (Dan) needed to replace the steps on the porch of our one-hundred-year-old home. I am not at all equipped to do home repair, but this seemed an easy task. With the risers secured in place by a more experienced friend, it was my job to cut the boards that would actually become the steps. I measured the length I needed, and cut the first board. It made perfect sense that all I needed to do was use the first one to place on top of the next board as a template to measure how long it should be, then draw a line and cut. I then used the second as a template for the third step, the third for the fourth and so on until all six steps were cut.

When I was done and stacked the six boards on top of each other to carry to the porch, it became instantly evident that each board I cut was longer that the one before. I should have cut each board with the exact measurement instead of hoping the previous board was representative of the true measurement.

This example can be applied to us as we look to others for a model, or template, of Christlikeness. It is tempting for those in the ministry to look at others who have achieved success. Whether it be the minister down the street from us or any of the famous ministers that can be seen on television, it is easy to find someone we wish we were like, or who has the type of ministry we would like to have. We run a great risk when we try to emulate our spiritual

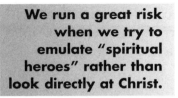
We run a great risk when we try to emulate "spiritual heroes" rather than look directly at Christ.

heroes as we attempt to be like Christ, rather than to look directly at Christ to see how He lived His life.

Paul encourages us, in Philippians, to imitate Christ's humility: "If you have any encouragement from being united with Christ, if any comfort from his love, if any fellowship with the Spirit, if any tenderness and compassion, then make my joy complete by being like-minded, having the same love, being one in spirit and purpose" (2:1-2). While having "spiritual heroes" can aid somewhat in our Christian walk, it is important that we don't dilute the example Christ set for us by modeling our walk after another person.

A Firm Adherence to a Moral Code: The Key to Healthy Leadership

Remaining True to What Is Right

As previously stated, we run the risk of impairing integrity when we dilute what we know to be right. This belief is also true in our role of leader in our church. Whether you are the senior minister in your church or the youth minister who oversees youth ministry, leadership is a key component of your job.

Some of the most difficult issues that ministers face are in the area of making wise decisions as they lead their congregation or their area of ministry. We've heard over and over that the biggest threat to doing what is right is often the challenge made by those in the church who—either by their history within the congregation or by the number of other members they have behind them—become a force to be reckoned with if things don't go the way they believe they should go.

When a church leader continues to allow a group of people within the congregation to have enough power to control his or her decisions (e.g., "Dare I use this example in my sermon because it might offend so-and-so" or "Can we change this worn-out tradition in our worship service, or will it offend so-and-so"), his or her integrity as leader is seriously impaired. While we are not suggesting a leader should always escalate conflict, a leader shows integrity when he is not afraid to do what is right, even if the consequence is having people angry with him, or running the risk of losing his job.

Many ongoing, multigenerational problems within churches would not have survived if the minister of the church nipped it in the bud early on. Not doing so **We don't suggest a leader should always escalate conflict, but integrity means not being afraid to do what is right.** leaves a legacy for years and ministers to come to attempt to deal with a problem that has grown exponentially because someone was afraid to deal with it.

But let's be honest with ourselves: there is plenty of blame to go around. Some congregations have been conditioned (or trained) by years of poor leadership, so it should be no surprise to us when people exhibit a negative reaction to change or are suspicious of leadership decisions. So how do we break this cycle? How do leaders remain true to what is right and build trust at the same time? When the leadership must make a tough decision, we need to ask two questions:

Is this a matter of personal preference?

Or is this a sin issue that needs to be confronted?

How we answer these questions affects how we minister to those in our care.

If this is merely a personal preference, what are our options? Can we reach a compromise? How can I, as a leader, model Christlike servanthood? Regardless if the problem is with someone in the pew or someone in a leadership role, we need to avoid the trap of thinking, "It's my way or the highway."

If this is a sin issue, the leadership should establish a plan to model Jesus' instructions in Matthew 18:15-17. Jesus calls for the same response, which pursues every avenue for possible reconciliation and the mending of relationships. We must learn to value relationships and accept the responsibility to hold others accountable for behavior that undermines Christian unity. It is often the failure of the church leadership to present a united front, which results in seriously weakening the discipline process.

This point leads to the next one:

When Dealing with People, Total Honesty Is Essential

We are familiar with the principle of leadership that states that one cannot lead people beyond the level he or she has attained. If this is true, or even partially true, how does this apply to church leadership? In George Barna's book, *A Fish Out of Water*, he states, "Believers whose faith is immature cannot be entrusted with the care of God's people, and those who cease to grow in their knowledge and relationship with God are insufficiently committed to Him to receive His trust and anointing." What is your reaction when you consider speaking this truth to those in your congregation? Does it inspire you, or strike fear within you?

We see from Scripture's example that ministry leaders should expect maturity from laity who serve in leadership positions. We can and should expect people to grow in faith and service and to be able to hear the truth and be challenged by it.

Telling the truth when dealing with people involves expecting fruit, as the proof and bounty of a mature relationship with Christ, from those under our leadership. Typically, what prevents this from happening is the minister who lacks wholeness and who has not addressed his own impaired condition which leads to fruitlessness as well. A minister who has not successfully examined his call (the second mark) and has not resolved the need to be liked by his congregation will have extreme difficulty telling the truth and expecting spiritual maturity from those under his care.

As stated previously, a church with a problem that has existed for numerous generations is usually the result of leadership that was unwilling to address the problem immediately when it arose. The surest way to put an end to this is to respond in total honesty whenever dealing with people. We have seen countless situations when the minister chooses not to tell a church member the truth because doing so might (or would) "hurt the person." The Apostle Paul wrote in his letter to the church at Ephesus (4:15), "Instead, speaking the truth in love, we will in all things grow up into him who is the Head, that is, Christ." Reconciliation and change have the best opportunity of happening when servant leaders speak the truth in love.

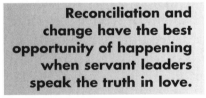

Reconciliation and change have the best opportunity of happening when servant leaders speak the truth in love.

Although this issue is pervasive, from supervising staff to volunteers, nowhere is it a bigger issue than when the minister or other church leader is in the role of counselor working with some-one in the congregation. Helping people to see the truth is one of the most powerful components of the counseling relationship. In a professional counseling relationship the counselor has little to lose when the one being counseled isn't happy with the truth brought to light through the counseling process. This is not necessarily true when the church leader is counseling someone who is a member of his or her church (as we discussed in the section about dual rela-tionships). We often avoid the truth because of the fear that telling someone the truth will lead to either that person leaving the church in anger or attempting to rally others to oppose the minister.

In chapter 3 we gave as an example a minister who was asked to perform the wedding of a friend from college. In premarital counseling it became apparent to the minister that the relationship was in trouble and that it was in the best interest of the couple that they postpone their wedding until each of them was in a healthier condition. This was very difficult for the minister involved, because telling the truth meant running the risk of losing his relationship with his friends. However, because he had a strong measure of integrity, he knew that consenting to performing the wedding would have cost him far more than the friendship. It would have cost him his integrity.

Telling people the truth is one of the most loving things we can do for them. However, it is equally important that we choose to tell people the truth because our integrity doesn't permit us to do otherwise.

Living above Reproach, but Not in a Glass House

A firm adherence to a moral code is easily summarized in this statement: Who we really are isn't necessarily evident when we are in public. Rather when we are alone and no one is watching, then the extent of our integrity is proven. Leadership places us in the spotlight whether we want to be or not. Although we suggest that healthy ministry leaders set boundaries around them in order to have private lives, it is not so they can be someone in private that they wouldn't want to be in public.

We want to convey the idea that a person of integrity who leads by a firm adherence to a moral code is the same person at home, on a business trip, in her financial dealings, behind the wheel of the car, in her private thoughts, or in a teaching position at church.

It's easier said than done. Expect it to be a struggle. Paul says in Romans 7, "I do not understand what I do. For what I want to do I do not do, but what I hate I do" (v. 15). To us there is no clearer picture of someone in the midst of the struggle for integrity. One wrestles with it daily and it is usually a very private strug-

> **Who you are in public needs to be who you strive to be in secret.**

gle. We are not suggesting that struggling privately leads to a lack of integrity in public. Rather, who you are in public—when you present your best self—needs to be who you strive to be in secret.

We have both been present when a minister decided that this secret struggle needed to be made public to the congregation for some reason (possibly relief from guilt through public confession or hope of accountability), only to walk away with nothing more than public humiliation. It is essential that we live our life as if we were under the microscope (or living in a glass house) without actually allowing our secret struggles to be given to the congregation. Rather, this should be shared with a sworn friend, a counselor, or trusted minister who can help with healing and provide accountability.

The Quality or State of Being Complete or Undivided: Wholeness

What better definition of "being whole" than "being undivided." There are countless things that seek to divide us, not only from others but also from ourselves.

First Things First: Setting and Maintaining Priorities

Learning to set a priority, then guarding and maintaining it, keeps our focus away from those things that lead to division. So many corporations and businesses have created vision or mission statements for their operations. Their reason for this is simple enough: a business that maintains its mission will be successful. For example, a company that has as its mission to produce the best tennis shoes on the market will simply have to consult its mission when presented with an idea to produce tap shoes. Manufacturing tap shoes would not help that business fulfill its mission. So it is with the many things in life for which we must find room in our time and hearts. We must consult our own ministry and personal mission statements when considering how to maintain priorities. Filling our lives and schedules first with things that do not further our mission does not leave enough room for the important things that do further our mission.

Establishing boundaries will aid significantly in clarifying what aids our mission and what does not. Church leadership, as a whole, should help hold each other accountable to individual mission statements. For example, if a youth minister has set as his department's mission statement that he will seek to present the gospel in a relevant way to junior and senior high students, then it becomes much easier for fellow church leaders to hold him in check when he takes on tasks that do not further that mission. When we take the time to filter our tasks and responsibilities, we are better able to maintain the correct priorities and balance in our personal and professional lives.

> **Filling our schedules first with what does not further our mission does not leave enough room for what does.**

Leading the Body to Oneness

When I (Dan) was a graduate student, I was required to address issues in my life that would impede my effectiveness as a therapist. The administrators of the counselor education program insisted that their students address and resolve their issues through personal therapy in order to complete the program and graduate. The reason behind this requirement was the belief that the counselor cannot take his or her client to any level of healing that the counselor has not been to. An added benefit is that the counselor who has become whole has a greater chance of inspiring his or her client toward health.

So it is with the ministry professional and his congregation. A minister who is not whole cannot lead the body to oneness. At the same time, a minister who is "whole" will find it essential that his congregation be whole. It can be very frustrating for the minister who finds his congregation unwilling to address those factors that lead to division.

If you're hoping this section will give you (in a few easy steps, of course) the way in which to avoid conflict and division within your church, you're going to be disappointed. It's difficult to see a church that is divided as being "whole." However, if you've been in the ministry for very long, you'll have to admit that it's rare to find a church that doesn't have some degree of division somewhere.

We propose that it is the process of *leading* the church to oneness that is important, not necessarily *achieving* oneness. We know that sounds like double-talk, but let us elaborate. Just as physical wholeness is an ongoing process, so it is when we explore wholeness within the congregation. If I go on a diet and begin an exercise regime that results in weight loss and greater physical shape, I cannot return to my old eating habits and laziness and expect the results to remain. Talk to anyone who strives for physical fitness. People will tell you that they're always just a few weeks away from returning to their undesired weight and level of fitness if they stop what they're doing. There's no room for complacency when it comes to health and wholeness.

While working towards oneness can be draining, it is essential that church leaders strive for it. Churches and their leaders will experience a degree of health just going through the process. A minister who takes the time to work on personal and spiritual wholeness will be better equipped to lead a church on the same journey.

Focus on Goals, Mission, and Task

How does being more concerned with the *process*, less concerned with *achievement*, really work in a church that expects results?

In the athletic arena, "Dance with the one who brung ya!" means that the player, or plays, that brought the team success are the same ones that should be used in the big game. Can this concept be applied to the ministry? What would it mean? Does it mean that the same sermons, the same gimmicks, and the same expectations that work in one church will work in another? Are the needs of one congregation in terms of growth the same in every other? Is church success measured universally?

First Corinthians 12:4-6 says, "There are different kinds of gifts, but the same spirit. There are different kinds of service, but the same Lord. There are different kinds of working, but the same God works in all men. Now to each one the manifestation of the spirit is given for the common good." Spirit, Lord, God—these are the ones responsible for gifts, service, and working/ministry.

Our nature leads us to believe that we are responsible for ministry results, both good and bad. Yet the previous Scripture clearly describes our "dancing partner" as the Holy Trinity.

> **We tend to believe that we are responsible for our ministry results, but our "dancing partner" is the Holy Trinity.**

Often earthly standards are used to measure the results in the church. We wonder if the church should really concern itself with the number of members, the amount of money, building campaigns, and the number of conversions and baptisms. Colossians 2:8 states, "See to it that no one takes you captive through hollow and deceptive philosophy, which depends on human tradition and the basic principles of the world rather than on Christ." We are cautioned in Romans 12:2 to "not conform any longer to the pattern of this world." We wonder if this still applies to the church today, which seems so much more interested in *achieving results* than *leading through process*.

How do the ministers of today's church respond without losing focus on the goals, mission, and task? In order to answer that question, we must decide who the "consumer" of today's church is. Consider this: McDonald's was on the leading edge when it developed the Super-Size meal—more drink, more fries, more food. The consumer wanted it, so McDonald's delivered. Decades later, when Subway began its campaign for healthier eating and the consumer agreed, McDonald's eliminated the Super-Size from its menu. This trend of becoming "consumer driven" has found a home in the American church as well. But we propose that the congregation is not the consumer. God is the consumer of our worship. Setting of goals, mission, and the task of the church must take into account what God wants.

We are expected to evangelize our world and we are expected to cultivate an environment in church that addresses the needs of those seeking. However, it is through worshiping Him and the work of His Holy Spirit that we are enabled to move to action in our local churches and the world.

We find no clearer statement of goal, mission, and task than in the great commission. "Therefore go and make disciples of all nations, baptizing them in the name of the Father and of the Son and of the Holy Spirit" (Matt 28:19). There is nothing herein that talks about appeasing the consumer, taking time to measure success, or worrying about the numbers on our membership database. It just tells us to go about making disciples.

To strive for wholeness in the body of Christ means that the minister has achieved some level of wholeness as well. Wholeness results as the body moves continually toward fulfilling the goals, mission, and task set before us by God. The minister who diverts his eyes from the distraction of *achievement* (earthly measures) and fixes a steady gaze on the task set forth by God not only leads those in his congregation to integrity, but also does not feel the weight of needing to prove his value through success.

In summary, the healthy minister *strives for wholeness* in his life and in his congregation, but is not concerned about *achieving success*. Paul, in his letter to the Philippians, describes his own inability to measure the success of his ministry: "Not that I have already obtained all this, or have already been made perfect, but I press on to take hold of that for which Christ Jesus took hold of me. Brothers, I do not consider myself yet to have taken hold of it. But one thing I do: Forgetting what is behind and straining toward what is ahead, I press on toward the goal to win the prize for which God has called me heavenward in Christ Jesus. All of us who are mature should take such a view of things" (3:12-15).

Conclusion

A Counselor's Perspective

"You sound so skeptical!" That's what I (Dan) have been told about the parts of this book that I have written. I admit that I can be skeptical of the church. I've been in the church my whole life and have been a member of nine different churches. I have been a therapist for nearly twenty years. Most of this time has been spent working in either a private Christian counseling center or in my current private practice. In addition to the numerous clergy who have sought my counseling services, I have counseled hundreds of Christians, many of whom have been wounded by the church, its leaders, or other unhealthy activities that have occurred in the church.

I have witnessed people being hurt in the churches I have attended. I find church and Christians in general to be very unsafe. However, from a desire to be obedient to God, I make church a major part of my life. It is essential for worship, growth, and fellowship.

A few winters ago, unbeknown to anyone in my family, our unvented, energy efficient propane fireplace was not burning properly. There was little evidence of this, at first. The flames appeared to be fine, it was warm, and there was not a noticeable odor. However, by spring we all began to notice the ceilings weren't as white. A grayish film covered everything in the house. Everything.

Inside cupboards, refrigerator, closets, and the farthest corners of the house were covered in this film. It was so pervasive it required a team of four adults an entire week of eight-hour days (and the cost of $5,000) to rid the house of the damage. It was amazing to my wife and me that we were so oblivious to what was being done in our home until it reached those proportions.

So it is in the church. I don't believe that most pastors set out to do damage to their congregations, their families, or themselves. Yet in an environment prone to sin (Satan's main targets are churches and ministers, especially if they are adding to the kingdom), a minister with unresolved personal and professional issues is likely to do more damage than good. Again, I don't believe that is always intentional, but a wound that is left untended typically becomes infected.

> **In an environment prone to sin, a minister with unresolved issues is likely to do more damage than good.**

It is up to you, the ministry professional, to ensure that this doesn't happen to your ministry. The first place to start is with you. Take responsibility for yourself and address the issues that can make you an easy target for Satan. This is the only hope for today's church.

I recently heard about a pastor who founded a church that has grown significantly in the last decade. He reached a point in his tenure where he felt squelched because the church leadership was not allowing him to make all the decisions or to get his way. His response was to leave that church and to start another one. In this new church he has been able to handpick the church leadership. He and his chosen leaders make all decisions for the church. Members are not allowed to vote.

I worry that this trend—those under the guise of serving God, while looking for the church to meet their need for power and an ego boost—will continue to plague the church. I implore you, the ministry professional, to take a serious inventory of your life and ministry. It will be to the betterment of not only your ministry, but also to your being.

A Minister's Perspective

I (John) have always responded well to direction. Tell me what to do, and I'll do it. Tell me how you want it done, and I'll do it that way. If I'm doing something wrong, tell me how to do it correctly and I'll fix it. The only area of my life where I resisted this pattern was when it came to taking care of myself. Although I usually look for the easy route, I learned with great difficulty that I had to take care of myself regardless how difficult the process was.

Ten years ago I was ready to leave the church where I have now served for nearly thirteen years. I was probably close to leaving the ministry entirely, though, at that time, doing so would have left me without an identity. I probably would have gone from church to church trying to find fulfillment.

What reason did I have given for wanting to leave? It would have been everyone else's fault, of course. The list would have contained *at least* these reasons:

- ☞ Too much conflict within the body
- ☞ Not enough response to my attempts to lead toward spiritual depth
- ☞ Not enough of them liked me
- ☞ I was not getting enough personal reward
- ☞ No one was listening to me
- ☞ Too much time at church, not enough time at home
- ☞ I couldn't keep everyone happy at the same time

Whew! I look back and realize now how close I may have been not only to losing my ministry, but also my family, my identity, and my relationship with God.

The process towards health has not been easy, and it's not completed. However, I can safely say in the past several years I've not felt the compulsion to run to another church where I believe the grass would be greener. My wife now has a husband and my children have a father whom they don't have to share with the church. Burnout is not looming over the horizon. I know who I am and strive to deepen my calling—a relationship with my Heavenly Father.

Dealing with the truth of my family of origin was probably the most difficult part of my healing, and at times it remains a painful reality. Although my family is still my family, they have resisted my attempts to have a deep, meaningful relationship. Instead they try to pull me back into the enmeshment that still defines their relationship.

> **I know who I am and strive to deepen my calling—a relationship with my Heavenly Father.**

It has been freeing to define myself in terms of *who I am*, rather than *what I do*. Originally this concept scared me. When I believed that I was called to the ministry (rather than called into a relationship with God), I always needed to be John-the-minister in order to feel that I had validity and purpose. To know that God wants a relationship with John-the-person gives me much greater security now.

Boundaries can still be very difficult to set and maintain, but I'm getting better at it. This has cost me some relationships in the church, as I no longer give people what they want if it's not healthy for them, or me. I admit that I still want everyone to like me but have also experienced the reality that you can't count on people who are only there for you when you're making them happy.

Allowing my true neediness to be exposed has undoubtedly been the hardest part of my healing. While I'm quick to say that I trust people, I have found that I really don't. It has taken a great deal of time and testing in a sworn friendship for me to allow the real me to come to the surface. This is an ongoing growth process for me, and the results are evident as I experience roots of security deepening.

Pastor, minister, missionary, chaplain—whatever your title is—until you accept the reality that you must deal with your own issues in life, you'll never be able to minister effectively. There's no way around it. I spent too many years telling myself that it was the church or individuals in my congregation that needed to change in order for me to be a success in the ministry. Through my story I have shown you that is not true. The choice is now yours.

Bibliography

Barna, George. *A Fish Out of Water.* Nashville: Integrity, 2002.

Blackaby, Henry T., and Kerry L. Skinner. *Called and Accountable.* Birmingham, AL: New Hope, 2002.

Cloud, Henry, and John Townsend. *Boundaries.* Grand Rapids: Zondervan, 1992.

Corey, Gerald. *Theory and Practice of Psychotherapy.* 2nd ed. Belmont, CA: Brooks/Cole, 1977, 1982.

Knierim, Neil, and Yvonne Burrage. *God's Call: The Cornerstone of Effective Ministry.* Nashville: Convention Press, 1997, 2003.

Powers, John S. *Surviving the Pastorate.* Retrieved September 2, 2004, from www.lifeway.com/pastor_cg020905.asp.

About the Authors

John Daniels serves as Associate Pastor for Christian Formation and Administration at First Baptist Church of Waynesville, North Carolina. He is a graduate of Carson Newman College, where he earned a bachelor's degree in Religion, and he also holds a master's degree in Religious Education from Southwestern Baptist Theological Seminary. He lives with his wife and two children in Waynesville.

Dan Yearick is a licensed professional counselor. He holds a bachelor's degree in Social Work from Roberts Wesleyan College and a master's degree in Counselor Education from The State University of New York College at Brockport. He currently maintains a private counseling practice in Waynesville, North Carolina, where he lives with his wife and three children.

A Shepherd's Guide to Counseling Fundamentals

Beth Robinson

A Shepherd's Guide to Counseling Fundamentals was written to help equip ministers to respond to the counseling needs of the members of the congregation in a godly and effective manner. While individuals frequently seek out ministers to assist with counseling issues, many ministers have limited training about counseling strategies and techniques.

In this book you will find an overview of the counseling process and the different types of counseling interventions. There is also a helpful glossary that provides a list of terms used in this book and terms that are commonly used in a counseling session to help the reader learn the language of counseling.

If you would like more information about this series please visit collegepress.com and click on the *Caring for the Flock* link.

90 pages, 4MA-694-9, $8.99

Lost & Found
Mark E. Jones

Everyone has been lost at one time or another; everyone has lost something of value.

When we experience the despair of lost character, lost direction, lost hope, Jesus steps in with real help and real answers. He did it when He walked the earth, and He still does it today.

In his newest book, Mark Jones looks at people in the Gospels who had each lost something of value, and then Jesus helped them find it. Through dramatic encounters with everyday people, Jesus reveals Himself as the answer for what's missing in our lives, whether it's a character trait, a proper perspective on life, or a purpose for living.

Also included in this book are great discussion questions making it an excellent source for small groups as well as for individual study. Do you know someone who could use a book to help restore hope, someone who feels like their past mistakes are insurmountable or their current situation is over-whelming? Lost & Found is a book about transforming your life one character trait at a time.

150 pages, 4MA-929-2, $12.99

POST CARD

Dear Lord,
Life sure is confusing.
Thanks for always being there,
Bill

Life Sure Is Confusing

Bill Putman

Life sure is confusing. It can also be painful and overwhelming.
Do you struggle with feelings of failure, inadequacy, or guilt?
Do you wish sometimes that you could start over?
God has done so much for us, but sometimes we can forget his sustaining mercy.

   In his book, *Life Sure Is Confusing,* Bill Putman shares insights, blessings, and stories of answered prayers, examples of God's mercy in the midst of some tough situations.

Table of Contents

- When you feel guilty and want to start over
- When it seems like God doesn't care
- When you can't forgive yourself
- When you don't want to forgive others
- When life seems hopeless
- When you feel inadequate
- When troubles overwhelm you
- When you are depressed and don't know why
- When your accomplishments don't satisfy
- When you are tempted to be immoral
- When it's hard to stay married
- When you don't love your mate anymore
- When you fail as a parent
- When your children are driving you crazy
- What to do while the rebel in your life is still running
- If you divorce . . .
- What I want to be like when I grow up

168 pages, 4MA-950-6, $11.99

Echoes of Heaven

Mark E. Jones

The Apostle Paul suggests that when the Holy Spirit lives inside of us, certain character traits become inevitable. Join Mark Jones as he takes you on an excursion in search of the echo of God for your own life through the examination of the Fruit of the Spirit. *Echoes of Heaven* is a fresh look at Galatians 5:22-23, both for individual study and small group interaction.

"Here is Biblical teaching at its best! Faithful to the text in a language all can understand. Every preacher and teacher will need this book to give windows to their sermons and lessons. Illustrations make a message come alive. Mark has been a close personal friend and has blessed my ministry. Those reading this book will learn what I have received from this author for two decades. It will bear fruit." — **Wayne B. Smith**

"Echoes of Heaven deals with some extraordinary issues to help us be more like Christ by developing the fruit of God's Spirit. It is so evident that Mark Jones is an excellent communicator with a heart for people and a knack for pertinent illustrations and applications. This book is a must-read for your small group, Sunday School class, or personal devotion time."
— **Bob Russell**, Retired Senior Minister
Southeast Christian Church, Louisville, KY

158 pages, 4MA-920-9, $9.99

Healing For a Bitter Heart:
Releasing the Power of Forgiveness

Charles R. Gerber

Harboring bitterness will slowly destroy a person's life and wreak havoc on relationships. If you struggle with the issue of forgiveness or if you know someone who does, this book is a must read. It will help you understand that truth and take steps to change your life for the better.

315 pages, soft, #4MA-787-2, $12.99

1-800-289-3300 · WWW.COLLEGEPRESS.COM